DATELINE
SOWETO

ALSO BY WILLIAM FINNEGAN

CROSSING THE LINE:
A Year in the Land of Apartheid

DATELINE
SOWETO

Travels with Black
South African Reporters

WILLIAM
FINNEGAN

PERENNIAL LIBRARY

HARPER & ROW, PUBLISHERS, New York
Grand Rapids, Philadelphia, St. Louis, San Francisco
London, Singapore, Sydney, Tokyo

For my parents

A portion of this book first appeared, in slightly different form, as "Getting The Story" in *The New Yorker*.

A hardcover edition of this book was published in 1988 by Harper & Row, Publishers.

First PERENNIAL LIBRARY Edition published in 1989.

Library of Congress Cataloging-in-Publication Data

Finnegan, William.
    Dateline Soweto.

    "Perennial library."
    Includes index.
    1. Finnegan, William—Journeys—South Africa—Soweto.
2. Journalists—United States—Biography. 3. Journalists
—South Africa—Social conditions. 4. Soweto (Africa)—
Social conditions.   5. Apartheid—South Africa—Soweto.
6. Riots—South Africa—Soweto.   I. Title.
PN4874.F45A3   1988   070'.92'4 [B]   87-46136
ISBN 0-06-091601-X(pbk.)

---

89   90   91   92   93   FG   10   9   8   7   6   5   4   3   2   1

Contents

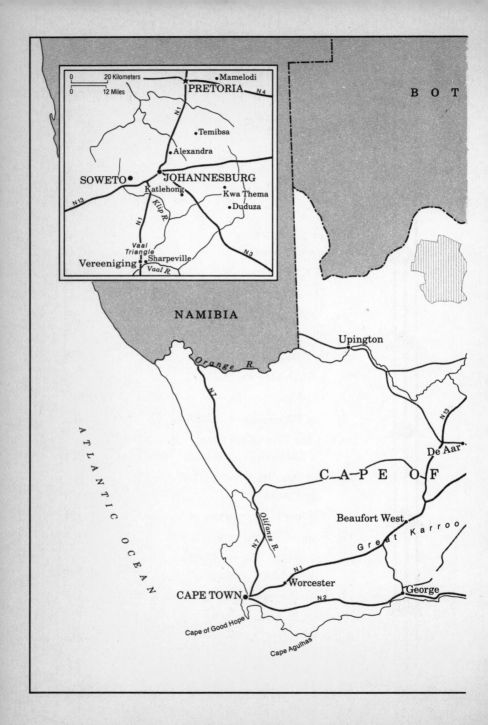

BOT

20 Kilometers

12 Miles

•Mamelodi

PRETORIA

N4

N1

•Temibsa

•Alexandra

SOWETO•

•JOHANNESBURG

•Katlehong

•Kwa Thema

N13

•Duduza

Klip R.

N1

Vaal
Triangle

•Sharpeville

Vereeniging•

Vaal R.

N3

NAMIBIA

Orange R.

Upington

N7

N13

De Aar•

C A P E   O F

Beaufort West•

Great Karroo

A T L A N T I C   O C E A N

Olifants R.

N7

N1

Worcester•

George•

CAPE TOWN•

N2

Cape of Good Hope

Cape Agulhas

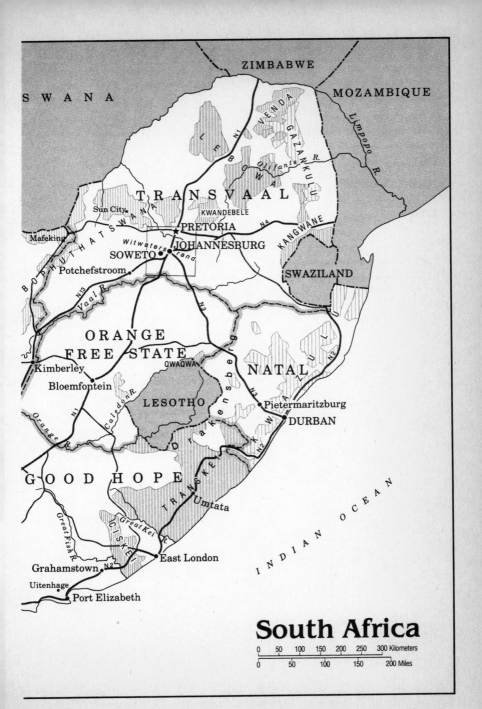

ZIMBABWE

SWANA

MOZAMBIQUE

VENDA

GAZANKULU

LEBOWA

Olifants R.

Limpopo R.

TRANSVAAL

Sun City

KWANDEBELE

Mafeking

PRETORIA

Witwatersrand

JOHANNESBURG

KANGWANE

SOWETO

Potchefstroom

SWAZILAND

Vaal R.

N13

N3

ORANGE
FREE STATE

QWAQWA

NATAL

Kimberley

Caledon R.

KWAZULU

N2

Bloemfontein

LESOTHO

Pietermaritzburg

Orange R.

N1

DURBAN

Drakensberg

N3

GOOD HOPE

TRANSKEI

Umtata

INDIAN OCEAN

Great Fish R.

Great Kei R.

CISKEI

East London

Grahamstown

N2

Uitenhage

Port Elizabeth

South Africa

| 0 | 50 | 100 | 150 | 200 | 250 | 300 Kilometers |

| 0 | 50 | 100 | 150 | 200 Miles |

Acknowledgments

This book sidled more than it marched into existence, and it received more than its share of help along the way. Mary Painter and Bryan Di Salvatore pointed me in the right direction. William Shawn gave me the wherewithal to do the reporting, and the confidence to give the story its head. In South Africa, I relied heavily on the kindness of Sylvia Vollenhoven, Robyn Rafel, Lauren Gower, Mike and Colleen Taylor, Hilary Saner and her family, Katharine McKenzie, and Aninka Claassens. Then there was the haven for writers provided by Harriet Barlow and Kaye Burnett at Blue Mountain Center in upstate New York, and the work of the Transvaal Rural Action Committee, the Surplus People's Project, and Eric Goldstein at the Committee to Protect Journalists. Among the books from which I have drawn, I want at least to mention *Total Onslaught: The South African Press Under Attack,* by William A. Hachten and C. Anthony Giffard (University of Wisconsin Press, 1984), and *Mabangalala: The Rise of Right-Wing Vigilantes in South Africa,* by Nicholas Haysom (Centre for Applied Legal Studies, Johannesburg, 1986). Bill McKibben, James Lardner, Lawrence Weschler, Tony Peckham, Daniel Ben-Horin, and Deirdre McNamer read *Dateline Soweto* in manuscript and made many valuable suggestions. At *The New Yorker,* my unwieldy work was improved immeasurably by John Bennet, Robert Gottlieb, Peter Canby, Hal Espen, and Eleanor Gould Packard. Next came Terry Karten, at Harper & Row, and Amanda Urban, my agent, who both saw the book in all this before I did. The debt of gratitude I owe to the many South Africans who took the time to talk to me will be obvious in the pages that follow—my greatest debt in this regard is to the reporters at the Johannesburg *Star,* whose willingness to share their world with me was truly remarkable. Finally, in the category of inexpressible thanks, there are my parents, Pat and Bill Finnegan, and the light of my life, Caroline Rule.

Freedom of the press is guaranteed only to those who own one.

—A. J. LIEBLING

Chapter 1

In KwaNdebele

Early July, 1986, was a bad time in KwaNdebele. It was an especially bad time to be lost in KwaNdebele. A state of emergency had been declared throughout South Africa the month before, suspending most of the country's few remaining civil liberties, and the emergency regulations for KwaNdebele—a small bantustan, or "black self-governing state," northeast of Pretoria—were particularly harsh. They barred all nonresidents from the territory and effectively placed KwaNdebele's 500,000 residents under house arrest between the hours of 9 P.M. and 5 A.M. A Johannesburg newspaper headline had declared KwaNdebele "A NO-GO AREA." But we had gone there anyway—Jon Qwelane, a reporter for the Johannesburg *Star*; Herbert Mabuza, a photographer for the *Star*; and I—and now we were lost.

I had wanted to bring along a map, but Qwelane had insisted we leave it in the city. "If they find that sort of thing on us, they'll just throw us straight in jail." Mabuza had said he knew the way to the mission station we wanted to reach, but it seemed that he had dozed past the junction. I drove swiftly down a two-lane highway, swerving to avoid goats and donkey carts and burned-out cars. Low hills of stony semi-desert, some of them covered with shacks and tents, all of them bone-dry in the rainless high-veld winter, rose and fell around us. Thorn trees grew in the gullies. We overtook a van and signaled the driver to pull over. The man's eyes popped when he saw me, a white man, driving. He pulled over. Qwelane went back to speak to him. Mabuza and I waited in the car, watching the rear-view mirror and chewing on the dried beef we had bought at a country store north of Pretoria. When Qwelane returned, he was shaking his head. "That poor guy was so scared he could hardly speak." Qwelane sighed. "He thinks it's back the other way."

I had been lost a lot over the preceding six weeks. I had been spending time with some of Johannesburg's black newspaper reporters, trying to understand something of what their lives were like, and one thing I had learned was that they spent a large part of their professional lives asking people for directions. Nearly always, their beats were the black townships and the bantustans—places not known for street signs or house numbers. Maps tended to be useless as well as dangerous. Black reporters and their drivers either developed remarkable powers of intuitive navigation or else they missed their deadlines. Just asking people for directions required special skills. Around Johannesburg, it had to be done in any of six or seven languages, and, in the extremely tense atmosphere of the past couple of years, it had to be done very sensitively. Black people's first assumption was always that strangers worked for "the system"—that is, the police. Strangers in cars were especially suspect, and the *Star*'s bulky Toyotas bore, in addition, an unfortunate resemblance to unmarked police cars (except under the hood, where they carried weak engines that the paper's black reporters hated with the fine passion of soldiers issued weapons that jam in combat). People tended to shy away from the cars, and even to bolt when one pulled up beside them.

The best way to get around was to have a local person, ideally a respected political activist, along as a guide. Arrangements were often made to pick up such a person en route to an interview or event. With me along, convincing strangers that we were not police was made even more difficult by the fact that I am white.

Black men and white men driving together in the townships are nearly always police. The drivers at the *Star,* who are black, would see me arrive in their basement garage with one of the black reporters, shudder, and immediately announce that they were all busy and we would have to drive ourselves. The only words I could understand in the ensuing arguments were "unrest" and "necklace" and "self-drive," but the problem was clear: the drivers considered it too dangerous to have me in their cars. When we showed up saying that we wanted to go to Kwa-Ndebele, the howls of "self-drive" were especially piercing. One old fellow kept running his finger around his neck, indicating the "necklace"—the gasoline-soaked burning tire used by angry mobs to execute suspected enemies. We couldn't spare the time to wrangle that day, which was why I was doing the driving as we wandered all over the blasted, frightening landscape of Kwa-Ndebele.

It looked as though a war had been fought there. The few shops we saw were all gutted. There were those burned-out cars. A beer hall fronted by a primitive arcade had large black tongues of charred paint licking up its turquoise walls from each arch of the arcade. More alarming than all the signs of recent violence, though, were the communities of KwaNdebele themselves. They seemed to be nothing but immense shantytowns, sprawled across the bare hills: a vast forest of poverty, with the houses packed as densely as in any urban township. Most of the houses were makeshift concoctions of cardboard, plastic, and corrugated metal. Many were simply packing crates with a door and a smoke hole cut out. Rocks anchored the roofs against high winds. Clearly, there was no electricity, no plumbing, no running water: everywhere, women and girls could be seen trudging down the dusty lanes with plastic water jugs on their heads. There were obviously no jobs in the area. Hundreds of thousands of people were marooned out in these huge bush ghettos. "And they wonder why we call this country a concentration camp?" Qwelane muttered. "These people truly have nothing left to lose."

KwaNdebele had put Qwelane, who was normally the most entertaining of men, in a terse, uncommunicative mood. In the

morning, he had been amusing Herbert and me with stories
inspired by the country we drove through: a yarn about children
who hate cabbage after we passed a truck full of cabbages; memories of various close calls on assignments in this district; a
rhapsody about the beauty of the eastern Transvaal. True, Qwelane's description of the eastern Transvaal, its flowers and wa-
terfalls and peaceful villages, had, after building to a climax of
bucolic images, hovered, and ended: "Then along comes a Boer
to spoil the whole effect." But that ration of grimness was there
in any black South African's view of his country. Now he
slumped in the back seat, drumming his fingers lightly on a slim
yellow box ("Mills: England's Luxury Cigarette"), chain-
smoking, and watching the landscape grumpily.

Qwelane had a reputation for being able to spot the
authorities—the police, the Army—and take evasive action before anyone else knew that anything was up. "You must be able
to sniff a cop in a crowd of a thousand people," he had once told
me. And I had seen him do it. But that was in town, where there
were crowds and alleys and doorways to duck into. His intimate
knowledge of every street in Soweto was of no use to us out here.
And even Qwelane had not always managed to elude his enemies.
He had a habit of turning his head to one side when others were
talking, for he had been deaf in one ear since 1978, when he
received a brutal beating from two off-duty white policemen.

Qwelane was thirty-three and looked older. From some angles,
his face reminded me of Nelson Mandela's—as Mandela appears
in photographs taken when he was over sixty. He had strong
cheekbones, narrow eyes, a small head, powerful shoulders, the
beginnings of a belly, milk-chocolate-colored skin, a sparse mustache, and a very sparse collection of chin whiskers. Qwelane's
father was Xhosa-speaking (their family name is pronounced
Kwe-LAH-nee, with a distinctive Xhosa "click" at the beginning),
and he is classified Xhosa under the apartheid system of racial
and ethnic classification, but his mother is Tswana, and Tswana
is his mother tongue. (Qwelane speaks six languages: Tswana,
Xhosa, Zulu, South Sotho, English, and Afrikaans.) Besides his

deaf ear, the marks of the kind of life he leads included a slight limp—the result of a gunshot wound that left him with a steel pin in his leg—and a missing left front tooth, which gave him a great raffish grin. On that day in KwaNdebele, he wore a well-cut gray-blue suit, with his necktie loosened in the manner of serious journalists everywhere. Except on weekends, I had never seen Qwelane in anything but a suit. It was one of the small things that distinguished him from his fellow black reporters, who all wore multipocketed canvas safari jackets, which they called lumberjackets.

Qwelane is the senior black reporter at the *Star*. Officially, he is on the staff of the *Sunday Star*—its only black reporter—and in that capacity he usually tries to "bank stories for the weekend," as he puts it. In practice, he works closely with the staff of the daily *Star,* and his stories often appear there, too. He enjoys an unusual amount of job freedom, partly because of his anomalous staff position, partly because of his seniority, but mostly because of his temperament. He is not known, to put it blandly, for his deference to authority. Indeed, Qwelane's editors had refused him permission to go to KwaNdebele, citing the danger and the official restrictions. That was why we had been in such a hurry to leave that morning—the editors were in a meeting and Qwelane wanted to be gone before they noticed he was missing.

The government's reluctance to have conditions in KwaNdebele exposed was understandable. This "self-governing state," which is somewhat smaller than Long Island, had been nothing but white-owned cattle farms until 1975, when the government began buying up land, but it had since become a major dumping ground for black South Africans displaced by a variety of causes, including the mass eviction of farm workers from their homes after the abolition of the tenant-labor system, the forced removal of black residents (including landowners) from areas designated for whites only, the persecution of non-Tswana residents in the Bophuthatswana bantustan, and the chronic, deliberate (it was part of government policy) shortage of housing and land in the urban townships.

The rationale for the bantustan system (over half of the 24 million Africans in South Africa* are now believed to live in bantustans) has always centered on the idea of ethnic states— each bantustan is the "homeland" of an African "tribe" and will eventually become that tribe's "country" as it achieves its "independence" from white-ruled South Africa—but KwaNdebele did not fit the rationale. The Ndebele-speaking people had no "homeland" in South Africa. After being defeated by the Boers in the nineteenth century, some fled across the Limpopo River to what is now Zimbabwe. Those who stayed behind were scattered through the Transvaal as indentured laborers on white farms. Nearly all the residents of what the government had decided was KwaNdebele had arrived in the area since the mid-1970s, and fewer than half of them were Ndebele-speaking. The residents of KwaNdebele were Zulus, Pedis, Vendas, Tsongas. I had seen an article about KwaNdebele in *National Geographic* a few months before which, while it didn't downplay the enormous problems faced by the bantustan's residents, did highlight the usual cast of bare-breasted maidens, young men celebrating their tribal initiations, and women in monstrous necklaces that deformed their collarbones. But if one wanted to see people in traditional Ndebele dress, or the fantastic Ndebele house painting, one really had to go further north, to the Lebowa bantustan. What brought people to KwaNdebele was not tribal identity but desperation and dispossession at the hands of the apartheid state. These great shack cities, which had sprung up virtually overnight, even bore bleak Afrikaans names: Kwaggafontein, Vlaklaagte, Tweefontein E.

The National Party government in Pretoria, undeterred by the fact that KwaNdebele is probably the least viable, politically and economically, of all the ten bantustans—four of which are already "independent," not one of which remotely resembles a

---

* The four main racial classifications in South Africa are African, "coloured" (mixed race), Indian (or Asian), and white. In this book, the term "black" will usually refer to Africans, but will sometimes include "coloureds" and Indians. In 1986, the population of South Africa, including the bantustans, was approximately 33 million—24 million Africans, 5 million whites, 3 million "coloureds," and slightly less than a million people of Indian descent.

country*—had recently decided to grant this tiny patch of rural misery independence. That was what all the fighting was about. Not everyone in KwaNdebele was enthusiastic about independence, which was scheduled for December 11, 1986. The burned cars we passed had belonged to Mbokodo, a vigilante group organized and armed by the bantustan authorities to impress upon the people of KwaNdebele the case for independence. The scorched and roofless huts we could see among the endless rows of shacks had been the homes of supporters of one side or the other.

The pro-independence faction was actually small. It comprised the few bantustan politicians and businessmen who stood to profit from independence, and their hirelings. People often say that a bantustan leader receives three things when he accepts independence: a sash of office, a palace, and a prison. A new prison and a new capital, complete with posh homes for the leaders, were, in fact, among the independence projects that Pretoria had promised the officials of KwaNdebele (along with a soccer stadium and a grandiose new legislative building, both of which were already under construction). More booty than that is available to those who administer bantustans, however, and much of it can be had with or without independence. The Chief Minister, Simon Skosana, and his cronies in the KwaNdebele Cabinet already controlled virtually every business enterprise in the area, from liquor sales to construction, and since they were also the sole distributors of business licenses, their hold on the local economy was in the way of being a death grip. As a group, they were not known for their sophistication—most of the Cabinet had been required by their masters in Pretoria to attend literacy classes, and Chief Minister Skosana, a former truck driver with five wives, had never finished primary school—but they had shown a certain cunning in their negotiations with the state over independence. In late 1985, they had received from Pretoria a large chunk of adjoining land for incorporation into

---

* All together, the bantustans, which are largely barren and, in every case, extremely poor, comprise only 13 percent of the total land area of South Africa. No country in the world except South Africa recognizes the bantustans, nor does the United Nations.

KwaNdebele. It seemed to matter not at all that most of the 120,000 residents of the area in question, known as Moutse, were Sotho-speaking and had no desire to be pushed into KwaNdebele. Moutse was comparatively fertile, prosperous country and its leaders had no leverage on Pretoria. Indeed, when the residents of Moutse objected to their annexation, they were visited by a large vigilante force led by members of the KwaNdebele Cabinet. The vigilantes, who were officially launched as Mbokodo a few weeks later, kidnapped more than four hundred men and boys, trucked them to a meeting hall in KwaNdebele, and tortured them for more than twenty-four hours. Chief Minister Skosana and members of his Cabinet personally oversaw the torture, which resulted in the death of at least two people and left many others maimed for life.

Resistance to the independence plan grew rapidly after that, not only in Moutse but throughout KwaNdebele. Students (there are around a hundred schools in KwaNdebele), workers, even teachers and civil servants began to express their opposition. Pretoria denied any connection with Mbokodo, but there were many reports that the South African security forces were working closely with the vigilantes. Pretoria had a great deal invested in KwaNdebele independence; the denationalization of as many black South Africans as possible remained, after all, the basic scheme for continued white-minority rule in South Africa. President P. W. Botha was said to be dealing personally with Simon Skosana. Mbokodo, in any case, had clearly been given a free hand to move against its critics. Youths were press-ganged into the vigilante ranks, and large detention camps were established, where captured opponents were severely tortured. Some were made to run across a yard of burning coals. No one knows how many did not survive.

The "comrades," as the youths among the anti-independence forces came to be called, started fighting back: boycotting their schools, holding mass meetings in the bush at night, and employing the necklace against their enemies. By May of 1986, KwaNdebele had turned into a killing ground. Much of what occurred there was what government spokesmen call "black-on-black violence," and the situation was indeed a perfect example of the regime's long-standing strategy for governing the black majority: provide scant resources, put a ruthless clique in control, and watch everyone else exhaust himself trying to wrest away that control—in a phrase, divide and rule. Yet the conflict in KwaNdebele had a focus—bantustan independence—that struck close to Pretoria's heart. As a result, journalists were harshly discouraged from covering events there, and when the June, 1986, state of emergency was imposed, a blanket of silence was thrown over KwaNdebele.

Originally, we had arranged to meet a group of comrades from KwaNdebele at the house of an activist in Pretoria. A Catholic missionary from the area was supposed to bring them to town. We had been looking forward to the meeting: the value of the story had been rising rapidly since we learned that the group coming to Pretoria would include a member of Skosana's Cabinet who was considering switching sides; a member of the Ndebele royal family, Prince James Mahlangu, who was opposed to independence; and Peter Skosana, Simon's eighteen-year-old son. Peter reportedly still had the scars on his face from a beating that had been administered by his own father's goons. He was said to be a leader of the comrades.

Alas, nobody had turned up for the Pretoria meeting but us. The activist tried for an hour to telephone the mission in Kwa-Ndebele. When she finally got through, the priest, who had recently spent several weeks in detention, told her that the entire party was still at the mission, that the Army was out in force that morning in KwaNdebele, that "a ring of steel" had been thrown around the bantustan for some unknown reason, and that they could not move. We asked if we couldn't try to come to them. The priest said that would be suicidal, apologized, and rang off.

We sat in disgruntled silence for a while. Finally, Qwelane finished his coffee, stood up, and said, "In that case, I think there is only one thing for us to do, gents."

Our hostess, a woman of documented courage, muttered, "Maybe another day."

Qwelane said, "Let's go to KwaNdebele."

*   *   *

If we had had the comrades with us, we would never have gotten lost. "But we would never have seen so much of this beautiful place," Herbert Mabuza said. "All this beautiful countryside. All these friendly people." Mabuza had a high, cheerful voice that somehow made sarcasm musical. His English had an educated ring to it, which was strange because he had never finished high school. He was a senior in Soweto at the time of the great student uprising of 1976. His involvement in student politics was rewarded, however, not with the appreciation of his community-mindedness by university admissions committees, but with eighteen months in solitary confinement. After his release, as Mabuza told it, he just sat around listlessly for a couple of years, "in some kind of shock." When he woke up, he got interested in photography, and he was soon one of the best black news photographers in the country. Mabuza was short, roly-poly, emotional, and a teetotaling Catholic. He wore wire-rimmed glasses and expensive-looking shoes and lived in Soweto with his parents, his wife, and his daughter. He liked to recall fondly the time he had spent working with Benjamin Bradlee, Jr., when he was in South Africa as a correspondent for the Boston *Globe*. Bradlee had commanded a budget that let them fly anywhere in the country on short notice and rent cars that did not look like police cars or deliver only half-hearted power in emergencies.

The people we asked directions from were not in fact unfriendly—they were just frightened, and not very helpful. One group offered directions that, after a few adjustments, did lead us to a Catholic mission. It just wasn't the right Catholic mission. The surprised nun we found there said we were at least twenty-five miles from our destination. When we got back to the highway, we passed a stack of tires for sale. The sight recalled one of the most bizarre provisions of the KwaNdebele emergency regulations, which outlawed the possession of "a motor vehicle tyre which is unfit for further use on a motor vehicle," and also of "any fuel not stored in the tank of a motor vehicle or other machine." The popular compliance with this "anti-necklace" regulation had been spectacular: the sky over the entire central Transvaal had been black with the smoke of burning tires.

Another emergency regulation specified, "No person may play, loiter or aimlessly remain on any public road or road reserve within KwaNdebele." I wondered if our behavior could be described as aimlessly remaining. I thought about some foreign journalists who had been picked up and jailed without charges in KwaNdebele earlier in the year, even before the state of emergency made their presence illegal, and about two people, one of them a black journalist, who had died in police custody in the nearby Lebowa bantustan in April. Mabuza and Qwelane may have been reflecting on similar matters, particularly after we passed a temporary Army camp for the second time. The dusty tents filled a small valley. Troop trucks, jeeps, barbed wire, khaki-clad figures, what looked like a helicopter—I hardly dared turn my white face toward the camp to look.

We started rehearsing our cover story. I was an anthropologist—no, a historian, researching the life of a local man who had become a saint. These were my assistants. "What state of emergency, sergeant?" "*Ja, baas,* we are the assistants." (Qwelane: "But that word"—he meant *baas*—"will stick in my throat.") The story didn't sound too solid this time through. Qwelane suddenly erupted. "Look at the way we're forced to operate! Sneaking around, making up stories for every situation that crops up. How can they expect us to do our jobs?"

In the end, we spent so long wandering around KwaNdebele, we got so punchy, that we forgot to be scared. We passed a bus and Qwelane and Mabuza pretended they were passengers reacting to the sight of us.

"Did you see that *umlungu*?"

"No, man, it was an albino."

"Yes, you must be right. What *baas* would let his natives ride like that, and in the front seat as well?" (Mabuza was scrunched down, with his feet up on the dashboard.)

Qwelane even found something good to say about the scarcity of street signs in the bantustans. Of a huge resettlement camp called Winterveld, in Bophuthatswana, he said, "All these contacts I've been making there will come in very useful one day. When I know the cops are looking for me, that's where I'm going to get lost. Much as they may want to find me, they will never succeed in there."

Late in the afternoon, as we were hurtling down a dirt road that looked exactly like twenty we had already traveled, Mabuza suddenly squawked, "There it is!" Off in a field we saw the mission.

The priest, whom I shall call Father Campbell, was astounded to see us. He was a tall, thin young man with troubled blue eyes. He took us into the living room of a low-roofed cinder-block house. The group we had wanted to meet in Pretoria had left an hour before, he said. There was no way to find them again today. He didn't know how we had made it as far as the mission without being stopped, especially with me in the car. He didn't know how we would get out of KwaNdebele. Whatever we did, we should not go any farther into the bantustan. Mabuza and I glanced at each other—we did not mention where we had spent the last four hours.

Qwelane asked Father Campbell if he would mind being interviewed. He said he wouldn't. A young woman brought glasses of beer for Father Campbell and me. Qwelane and Mabuza had coffee. There was a tiny chapel off the living room. Across a field we could see the mission church—a converted sheep shed, built of tin and painted red, with a crude white cross painted on one wall. Qwelane asked Father Campbell if the news of recent events in KwaNdebele had been reaching the outside world.

The priest shook his head wearily. "We estimate that the government has reported only a quarter, if not a fifth, of the real number of deaths in KwaNdebele since the beginning of the state of emergency. We estimate that there have been at least a hundred people killed here since May 13th. The average right now is about two a day. I have found, or gone to see, many of the corpses myself. And, except for the time that I was in jail, I have kept a record."

Father Campbell showed us a small leather-bound book. It looked like a missal. He went on, "I can usually tell by the wounds who did the killing. R-1 rifles are the Army. So are rifle-butt beatings. Pistols and sjamboks"—a sjambok is a metal-tipped whip—"are Mbokodo. Burned is the comrades. When people find a body or suspect a killing, they call me, and I go and look for it, and record the particulars. Mbokodo has been quiet since June 12th, when they attacked Tweefontein. I don't know how many they killed that day. I know I buried five. But Mbokodo has been on the run lately. Those members who are still in their houses are being guarded by the Army. Even the local KwaNdebele police don't like them anymore. The police stood by while the comrades burned Mbokodo shops. The comrades rule here now. They meet in houses by day, in the bush by night. They want to go back to school, mainly because it's easier for them to organize there, but their demands for ending the boycott are not likely to be met. They want Mbokodo disbanded, the troops out of KwaNdebele, and all detainees released. There are hundreds of comrades in detention."

I wondered about Father Campbell's own time in detention, but he seemed more interested in the plight of the people of KwaNdebele. He had been at the mission for several years, and had seen the area go from a pre-political backwater to the front lines of the South African revolution. "The ideology of the comrades is simple. They are anti-independence, anti-Mbokodo. There are no affiliated politics here yet. It's still a united ideology, and everybody shares in it. You talk to any old *gogo*"—grandma—"ask her about independence, and even she's against it. You'll go a long way here before you find anyone who's for independence."

Father Campbell surprised us by describing Simon Skosana as "an inoffensive puppet." He said, "The real problem is the man who controls him—Piet Ntuli, the Minister of the Interior. He is the really greedy, the really bloodthirsty one. A lot of people here think that there will never be peace until Ntuli is eliminated."

We had heard of Piet Ntuli. He was one of the richest men in KwaNdebele, and he ran some of the most notorious rackets there. He had faced many criminal charges—for large-scale auto theft, hoarding of weapons, and, in two cases, murder—but had never been convicted. Ntuli had led the vigilante raid on Moutse. It was said that he had flogged to death a number of comrades. It was hard to read Father Campbell's attitude toward the idea of Ntuli's being "eliminated."

When I asked him about his influence with the comrades over their tactics, he shrugged. "I've stopped them from necklacing three people lately, purely because I came along at the right moment and managed to talk them out of it," he said. "One was a boy whose *father* was in Mbokodo. I managed to convince them that he could not be held responsible for that. Another was a boy who had tried to rob a girl by stabbing her in the eyes." Father Campbell sipped his beer and looked bleakly out the window. He went on, "It has become quite hard to know who is doing what now. There was a boy who was shot by the Army. We saw him loaded into the ambulance. And then he simply disappeared. There are no hospitals in KwaNdebele, so I went around to the hospitals in the farming towns nearby, but he just wasn't in any of them. They said they had never heard of him. So I started going around to the mortuaries. And I couldn't believe the number of unclaimed bodies I saw, everywhere I went. At one place, I found sixteen necklace victims from the previous two weeks. And I don't believe those necklacings had been done by the comrades."

This, I had heard, was a grisly new wrinkle in a number of areas: secret necklacings by vigilantes and the security forces, which were subsequently blamed on the resistance.

Qwelane was taking notes. We were getting a story after all. At the beginning of the interview, he had turned to me and said, "Let's commit as much of this as possible to memory." Then, after a minute, he had emptied a box of cigarettes and started writing inside the box. He questioned Father Campbell about dates and names, and scribbled while Campbell read from his leather-bound book. When the cigarette box was covered with writing, Qwelane carefully replaced the foil and the cigarettes. He went on taking notes on scraps of paper, and when the scraps were covered he stuffed them in his socks. He pursued every detail about the boy who disappeared after leaving in the ambulance, including the boy's mother's approximate whereabouts in Kwaggafontein. Then he murmured to Mabuza, "Sidebar."

Father Campbell seemed to be catching some of Qwelane's enthusiasm for getting out the story about KwaNdebele. He went to a back room and returned with a slim young man in a ragged sweater, whom he introduced as Vusi. Vusi was a comrade, hiding from the police. He told us that he had been forced to join Mbokodo after a severe sjambokking, and had gone along on several raids before he was able to defect. "I was fortunate to be accepted by the other comrades," he said. Others had been necklaced despite having left Mbokodo. Vusi was nineteen years old. He said he wanted to return to high school. "But Skosana must first finish Standard Five," he said, giving us a shy smile. "That is one of our demands."

Vusi had a grandmother in KwaThema, a township near Johannesburg. I asked him why he didn't stay there.

"There is fighting there as well," he said. "And not only the cops are after us but the other side. Here, at least the struggle is united." That the resistance was splintered in many townships, and spent more time in internecine fighting than in opposing Pretoria, was not news, but that anyone would want to flee that frying pan for the fire of KwaNdebele seemed insane. And yet Vusi had a wild intensity about him that I had seen in other comrades—a consciousness of mortality brought prematurely to the surface. He began to talk politics, in an abstract way that verged on the visionary and that I found claustrophobic. "We only want peace," he said, his dark eyes fixed on mine. "We only want the end of this oppression, so that we may all be equal in the land of our birth, and love one another as brothers."

The sun was going down; it was time for us to go. Qwelane made arrangements with Father Campbell to see him later in the week, along with Peter Skosana and Prince James Mahlangu. As we were leaving, three more comrades, scruffy boys in T-shirts, showed up. We left Father Campbell sitting at his kitchen table carefully taking down a complicated story of police harassment, which the boys were telling him in Ndebele. He said he would pray that we met no Army roadblocks.

After two or three tense minutes while I tried to start the Toyota with what turned out to be the key to the trunk, we got away from the mission. It was dusk, and the highway, which had been almost empty earlier, now carried an unbroken stream of powder-blue buses returning from the cities. The majority of KwaNdebele's workers commute to jobs in "white South Africa." Some of them travel more than a hundred miles each way, spending eight hours on buses every day. Women leave their families four hours before daylight to be able to serve white families in Pretoria their morning tea in bed. Black workers can't possibly pay the market rate for so much long-distance transport, so the government, having forced the workers to live so far from their jobs, is itself forced to subsidize the bus service on a large scale: apartheid social planning at its most absurd. The explosive population growth in KwaNdebele has, in any event, provided Putco, the bus company, with a windfall. Where two regular buses ran in 1979, 263 were running five years later.

The exhaust pouring out of the buses as they ground over the low hills darkened the air as we drove toward a brilliant highveld sunset. Mabuza, inspired, disclosed an ambition. After the revolution, he said, he wanted to be the general manager of Putco. He would improve conditions so dramatically that people would be amazed.

Qwelane watched the road behind us for headlights.

It was hard to tell exactly where we were. Then we saw the silhouettes of a row of towering sisal stalks, which we recognized, and we knew we were out of KwaNdebele. The atmosphere inside the car turned instantly festive.

Qwelane talked enthusiastically about the story he would write. "I'll ring up Peter Reynolds—he's the paper's lawyer—first thing tomorrow morning, and see what he thinks we can say. I suppose I'll have to talk to old Skosana, get his side of the story, although his goons are very wary of the press. I once tried to ask him some questions, and his henchmen just wouldn't allow it."

"I'll ask him for a family portrait," Mabuza said, laughing.

Conversation turned to the subject of fathers and sons. Qwelane's wife had just given birth to their second child, and he was concerned that their firstborn, who was nearly two, might become jealous of his new sister. "I think I will start taking him around with me when I go visiting," he said, and then he suddenly cried, "Look there, it's a new moon! My daughter was born on the new moon!" A sliver of moon hung before us, about to follow the sun down. "We should call her Tebogo," Qwelane said, adding, for my benefit, "It means 'Blessings from the Lord' in Sotho." I didn't see the connection between the name and the new moon, but it was that kind of moment: exuberant, thankful, adrenaline-giddy—a mood to name children in.

We were hungry, but stopping at a restaurant in Pretoria was not an option for two blacks and a white. We reached the *Star*'s offices, in downtown Johannesburg, sometime after ten. The transport manager exclaimed when he saw us pull into the garage—he had given us up for lost.

Upstairs, the newsroom was deserted. Mabuza stashed his cameras—he had not used them that day—and left for home. Qwelane went to a computer terminal in a corner. He called up his "desk"—his personal file—on the monitor and studied the messages that had been left there since the morning. Then he got out his cigarette box, dumping the cigarettes and the foil liner on the desk, and pulled the scraps of notepaper from his socks. He said he wanted to enter his notes before he forgot what "all these hieroglyphics" meant. When he was finished, he would walk over to the bus stand in west Johannesburg, where he would catch the first of three taxis he had to take to reach his house in Soweto.

Chapter 2

The Apartheid Press

In the ragged, slow-motion revolution that convulses South Africa, black journalists play a critical role. Their beat is the war zone: the townships and bantustans. It is virtually impossible for white reporters to cover the fighting. They don't speak the languages that are essential for getting around. The complexities of black politics and black society—not to mention the intricacies of township geography—are really comprehensible only to those who live among them. Also, of course, simply being white in a black township today is dangerous. Thus, local black reporters are often the only source of accurate news about the conflict in South Africa. The government is aware of this fact, and spends a great deal of time and energy harassing black journalists—jailing them, "banning" them, interrogating and torturing them, and closing down black community newspapers.

I had wanted to spend time with black reporters on a white liberal paper—the *Star* is such a paper—because their position seemed to me extraordinarily complex, placing them, as it does, among so many conflicting forces: the police, their editors, the paper's owners, and, above all, the black community, which is itself a complex network of competing political and economic forces.

Like the society as a whole, the press in South Africa exhibits an impressively divided personality. People like to say that one must read half a dozen different newspapers to have any idea what's going on in the country. Linguistic differences alone account for some of this fragmentation; South Africa has two official languages (English and Afrikaans) and nine or ten other languages are widely spoken. Of course, the press also reflects its owners: the country has twenty-five major daily and weekly papers, and each of them can be clearly identified with one of the country's two dominant white groups. There is no tradition of non-aligned newspapers in South Africa—no paper that can plausibly claim to be even its region's paper of record, let alone the nation's. Ethnic diversity aside, the political terra firma on which such a centrist institution could be constructed does not exist.

The Afrikaans-language press, which consists today of six major dailies and one national Sunday paper, had its origins, during the early years of this century, in Afrikaner political aspirations. Papers were launched not as commercial ventures but as organs of the National Party. They often carried little or no hard news; their editors were politicians, not journalists. The Afrikaans press played a crucial role in the National Party's rise to power, in 1948, on a platform it called apartheid. The first Nationalist Prime Minister, D. F. Malan, had previously been the editor of Cape Town's *Die Burger,* and H. F. Verwoerd, perhaps the most influential of Malan's successors as Prime Minister, had previously been the editor of Johannesburg's *Die Transvaler.* (Both men were Dutch Reformed ministers before becoming editors. Not surprisingly, neither distinguished himself as a newsman.) All the Afrikaans newspapers are owned by prominent National Party members, and their boards of control were until recently dominated by Nationalist cabinet ministers. In the last few years, the companies that own the papers have shown their first profits ever, but these are usually attributed to the lucrative government printing contracts—for telephone directories, school textbooks, and the like—that the companies are routinely awarded.

Also in the last few years, some Afrikaans newspapers have occasionally shown a small but unprecedented measure of editorial independence from the government, reflecting the intense debates taking place inside the National Party over "reform." And the two big Afrikaans publishing companies, Perskor and Nasionale Pers, are in fact associated with different wings of the National Party—Perskor with the party's Transvaal branch, Nasionale Pers with the Cape Nationalists led by P. W. Botha—and are surprisingly bitter rivals. Still, the Afrikaans newspapers address themselves exclusively to the ruling white Afrikaner community. Virtually no one else reads them, and other South Africans tend to see them as little more than government mouthpieces. (Actually, they are sometimes much more than mouthpieces. In 1986, the Johannesburg morning daily, *Beeld,* was discovered by the *Observer* of London to be actively collaborating in the government's campaign to get the African National Congress, South Africa's leading black-liberation movement, expelled from its offices in Britain. The *Observer* found that *Beeld* had been plotting to smear the ANC by secretly monitoring meetings in London between an ANC representative and a British gunsmith during which the gunsmith attempted to sell arms to the ANC. *Beeld,* whose editors were in cahoots with the gunsmith, planned to expose any sale, and thus increase the pressure on the British government to throw out the ANC.)

The one pro-government English-language paper, the *Citizen,* of Johannesburg, was launched with secret government funds as part of an ambitious domestic and international propaganda campaign in 1976. After the sources of its financing were exposed in the Information Department scandal of 1978, the *Citizen* was hastily bought by Perskor. Although its editorial line did not change, and its advertising-to-copy ratio suggests an ongoing financial hemorrhage, the *Citizen* has somehow survived, confounding widespread expectations that its credibility problem would prove terminal. Today the *Citizen* reigns as the only general-interest English-language morning paper in Johannesburg. Its tone is shrill, its format tabloid, and its small staff worked like drayhorses, despite the paper's heavy reliance on

wire-service stories to fill its pages. The *Citizen,* like the Afrikaans papers, supports P. W. Botha's government in virtually
everything it does—its nickname among journalists is "the Government Gazette"—and usually appears to be addressed to an
entirely white readership.

Radio and television in South Africa are state-controlled. Television was only introduced in 1975, after years of resistance to
the idea from the leaders of the Dutch Reformed Church, whose
influence in the National Party and the government is almost
impossible to overstate, and who feared the moral decay, corruption, and subversive foreign ideas they expected TV to bring.
Radio is broadcast on sixteen channels, in a variety of languages.
Until recently, television was a whites-only affair, broadcasting
half in Afrikaans, half in English, though three channels for
blacks have now been added, broadcasting in vernacular African
languages. The South African Broadcasting Corporation, which
runs both TV and radio, is intimately associated with the National Party. Its top officials are all members. In fact, they are
usually taken directly from the ranks of the Broederbond, a
semi-secret Afrikaner leadership group to which every prime
minister since 1948 has belonged. Although the SABC is ostensibly independent of direct government control, its true status
sometimes appears even in the statements of government officials. Once, P. W. Botha was threatening the opposition press
with further curbs, during a speech in Parliament, and mentioned that he would, for his part, be ordering the SABC "not to
headline subversive or revolutionary elements."

No one has ever accused the SABC of giving prominence to
such elements. Indeed, the picture of South African life available
on South African TV and radio seems to bear only the most
distant resemblance to what is actually happening in the country.
American sitcoms and series (often dubbed into Afrikaans or an
African vernacular) predominate on TV—*The A Team* and *The
Cosby Show* are current favorites—and news reporting is selec-
tive and tendentious, customarily presenting only the government's view of events while attacking or ignoring its opponents.
Most of those opponents consider the SABC to be worse than

useless as a news service, though I have also heard claims that certain programs offer inadvertent but helpful forecasts of the state's intentions. For example, immediately after a morning radio program called *Comment* attacked Dr. Allan Boesak, the anti-apartheid leader, for two days running in 1985, Dr. Boesak's home was raided and he was jailed without charges. Again, in May, 1986, *Comment* broadcast a host of accusations against some of South Africa's neighbors. Within days, the South African military had launched bloody raids against Zimbabwe, Zambia, and Botswana.

Within a divided press like South Africa's, there is often no agreement even about what constitutes news. On June 20, 1986, for example, P. W. Botha gave a speech at a graduation parade at the South African Police College in Pretoria. The Afrikaans press covered the speech in great detail, with some papers running page-one photographs of the State President. The TV evening news devoted considerable time to the speech. And the next day's *Citizen* outdid itself, running no fewer than four stories. One, headlined "PW WARNS AGAINST NEW PUBLIC HOLIDAY IDEALS," spelled out the dangers of the "new holidays which some people in South Africa want to introduce." A second story, headlined "CUBANS BLOCK PLAN FOR SWA," blamed the Angolan government for South Africa's failure to implement the UN Security Council's resolution on Namibian independence. Like the holidays story, this was wire-service fare from the South African Press Association and, again like the holidays piece, one had to read into the second paragraph to discover that the story was actually drawn entirely from the Police College speech. Then there was a straightforward article, signed by "Citizen Reporter," about the graduation parade, describing the ceremony and listing which awards Botha presented to whom and for what. Finally, there was a long, bylined piece with a large, bold headline: "PW TELLS POLICE OF 'THE GREAT LIE' ABOUT SA." This piece carried highlights from the State President's speech. "Our enemies latched onto the word 'apartheid' and in a sly manner transformed it into the strongest weapon in the onslaught against freedom and civilization in our country. A carefully calculated propaganda game is unfolding against us internationally and even internally, specially with the assistance of some of the media," Botha said, clearly not thinking of the *Citizen.*

I watched the Police College speech on a television in the *Star* newsroom with a group of *Star* reporters and editors. They laughed at some of the more histrionic lines ("You stand in the front line against the forces of communist enslavement and crime," the State President told the new policemen) and at the figure Botha cut with his small black homburg perched on his large bald head. The next day's *Star* did not run a line of the Police College speech. None of the opposition papers did. As far as they were concerned, there had been nothing new or noteworthy in it.

It is one of the peculiarities of the South African scene that, although Afrikaans-speaking whites outnumber English-speaking whites three to two, the English-language newspapers dominate the press, even among whites, accounting for three-quarters of daily circulation. There are about twenty of them, and they are the largest and most successful papers and always have been. What is especially peculiar is that, while a sizable majority of whites, including many English speakers, support the Nationalist government, the English-language papers (except for the *Citizen*) have consistently opposed it, often vociferously. In fact, the English press was responsible for uncovering the Information Department scandal, which brought down some of the highest figures in the National Party, including the then Prime Minister, B. J. Vorster.

The *Rand Daily Mail* of Johannesburg was, until its demise in April, 1985, the flagship of the English press and, it is safe to say, the government's least favorite newspaper. There are many explanations for the death of the *Mail,* but mismanagement is never far down anyone's list. The South African newspaper industry has been shrinking for the past decade, largely owing to losses of advertising to television. Two companies own all but a handful of the English papers, and the smaller of the two, South African Associated Newspapers, which was the *Mail*'s owner, has had chronic financial problems. The larger company, the Argus

Printing and Publishing Company, continues to field nine major papers, six of them dailies, and to show a healthy profit. The Argus Company's largest and most successful paper—the largest and most successful daily in South Africa—is the Johannesburg afternoon paper, the *Star*.

The *Star* was actually founded in Grahamstown, in the eastern Cape, in 1871 as the *Eastern Star,* and moved to Johannesburg in 1887, only one year after the city itself sprang into existence on the site of the great Witwatersrand gold strike. Its early financial backers were the British-owned mining houses of the Witwatersrand; its first readers were the British miners who flocked to the region to seek their fortunes. Since both of these groups had fierce differences with the government of the time— the old Transvaal Boer Republic, which insisted on treating them as rightless aliens—the *Star*'s role as critic of Afrikaner rule was established immediately. The paper was even implicated in an abortive British coup in 1897, and as a result was briefly shut down by the Boer authorities. The tensions between British and Afrikaners culminated in the Anglo-Boer War of 1899–1902, and there are those who say that the *Star,* in its opposition to the present government, is basically still fighting the Boer War. (The English-language press has actually been the nemesis of conservative Afrikaners since the first newspapers were established in the Cape Colony in the 1820s. The "liberal, philanthropic, independent press" was even blamed for driving a large band of early Afrikaners out of the Cape in 1834 on what became known as the Great Trek. This celebrated expedition of conquest and settlement in the African interior is more often seen, however, as a response to the abolition of slavery in the Cape.) Tensions reached another sort of pitch during the Second World War, when many Afrikaners, including H. F. Verwoerd, the future Prime Minister, were pro-German. After the *Star* ran an editorial, early in the war, attacking Verwoerd's paper, *Die Transvaler,* for publishing Nazi propaganda, Verwoerd sued for defamation. He lost the case, as the court found that "he did support Nazi propaganda, he did make his paper a tool of the Nazis in South Africa, and he knew it," and he was later jailed for the duration of the war. Today, some of the changed terms of the conflict between the English-language press and Afrikaner nationalists are perhaps reflected in the penchant among government supporters for referring to the *Star,* with the Manichaean humor they favor, as "the *Red Star.*"

The *Star*'s editors call constantly, in columns and editorials that are often eloquent, for an end to apartheid, and for immediate negotiations between the government and the leaders of the black majority. The paper's position is not always subtle. A recent page-one headline fairly roared, "FREE MANDELA NOW." The story beneath turned out to concern a demand by leading South African businessmen for the release of the jailed leader, but the *Star*'s endorsement of the demand was lost on no one. Whether the *Star* has been able to fill the *Rand Daily Mail*'s shoes, politically and journalistically, is a much-debated point. Rex Gibson, the acting editor-in-chief of the *Star* while I was around, and a former editor of the *Mail*, says simply, "We have become the lightning rod."

At first glance, the *Star* looks like any British provincial evening paper. Color photographs and bright three-color ads for supermarket specials on Rhino Table Salt flank serious coverage of national and international news. The paper has a substantial business section, and a very substantial classified section, particularly on Saturdays, when the Property Supplement runs. The *Sunday Star* is two hours' reading for the moderately conscientious, and comes complete with a magazine. But, with a closer look at the domestic news, the *Star*'s homely familiarity dissolves. The staple stories and master images belong to a William Burroughs nightmare: restless natives, police snuffing out pockets of resistance, a daily stream of truly Fascist ministerial pronouncements. And this dark fare seems to spill its menace across the ads for fish, beer, duvets, lounge suits, microwaves, the "Maxiciser Home Gym," the pet-advice columns, the brief, affected book reviews. In this unsettling context, the fine cadences of principled opposition nearly always to be found on the *Star*'s op-ed pages, along with the contributions of the paper's black reporters—their African surnames fairly dancing on the bylines—are a special relief: beacons in a racist darkness, sweet reason in the midst of major madness.

Overseas visitors to South Africa are invariably struck by the vigor and quality of the English-language press. In truth, the press is much freer to express opinions than it is to report facts. Censorship is a major feature of the South African political and cultural landscape. Thousands of books, films, magazines, and plays have been banned by the Nationalist government, for reasons ranging from the obvious to the incomprehensible. Journalists contend with close to a hundred laws restricting what they may report and with a fearsome array of measures that the government may take (and has taken) against journalists, including arrest and incarceration without charges, prosecution under a slew of sweeping security laws, and arbitrary "banning"—the peculiarly South African punishment, inflicted by the Minister of Law and Order, that amounts to erasing a person from society, with no reasons ever given. Banning orders usually run from two to five years, always forbid a journalist to work, and always include some form of house arrest; the practice has been described as "a jail sentence carried out without the expense to the state of feeding and housing the prisoner." Newspapers may not quote a banned person, or publish almost anything about the South African military, prisons, nuclear industry, or security police* without official permission. A book called *The Newspaperman's Guide to the Law,* a 332-page litany of peril, written by a lawyer, is to be found on virtually every working reporter's desk (every reporter in the opposition press, that is—no one working on a government paper, or in television or radio, has, to the best of my knowledge, ever been prosecuted). What is more, all these laws represent press restrictions under "normal" conditions. Under the current state of emergency, extensive new curbs have been introduced.

Probably the most insidious press censorship of all, however, is self-imposed. For more than twenty years, no South African

---

* Sometimes known as the Special Branch, or the Security Branch, this plainclothes wing of the police deals only with "political" crime. Its size is a state secret, but its power has grown immensely in recent years.

newspaper dared to quote Nelson Mandela; then someone noticed
that it was apparently not illegal to do so. The scope of the laws
is often vague and arbitrary, and the perpetual uncertainty about
what will be allowed leads to even more caution than is necessary.
Thus, self-censorship is more effective than official censorship,
which at least can't restrict expression it hasn't foreseen.

All the uncertainty is exacerbated by a widespread (and quite
justified) suspicion among reporters that they are being watched.
The police routinely tap the telephones of journalists—including
those at the *Star*, Rex Gibson assured me—and, by the Minister
of Law and Order's own admission, have informers in place in
every English-language newsroom. "No journalist should be surprised or disappointed about that," Louis Le Grange, then Minister of Law and Order, told the Committee to Protect Journalists
in 1983. "No journalist of any experience should try to bluff me
and say that's not to be expected." Rex Gibson once suggested,
only half-jokingly, to the Commissioner of Police that they really
should stop double-paying certain members of the *Star*'s staff,
but the effect of this situation on newsroom morale and professional solidarity is, of course, no joke. Neither does Jon Qwelane
laugh when he talks about what he calls "The Pretenders"—
police who masquerade as reporters and TV news crews, filming
meetings and funerals and otherwise "making our job more dangerous than it already is."

Direct intimidation is also used at a surprisingly high level.
The editors of all major newspapers are regularly compelled to
attend meetings, called by the Cabinet or the police or both, at
which the government makes known its views about the proper
role of the press in combatting the "revolutionary onslaught" it is
convinced it faces. That role does not include knowing a great
deal about the government's operations. There is no Freedom of
Information Act, or anything resembling it, in South Africa.
There are, however, laws that require reporters to check any
story concerning police actions with the police themselves, with
the result that reporters spend an appalling amount of their time
waiting for telexed replies to their telexed inquiries to police
headquarters in Pretoria.

* * *

Although the South African mass media have always catered primarily to white needs and interests, and reflected white views and values, the majority of the country's newspaper readers, radio listeners, and television watchers (not to mention people) are black. There is no black-owned general newspaper in South Africa, but there are a number of papers directed exclusively at black readers. The major black papers in Johannesburg are the *Sowetan,* an Argus-owned daily with a circulation of 120,000; *City Press*, which is owned by Nasionale Pers and puts out two editions a week, with a circulation of about 160,000; and *New Nation,* a church-owned bi-weekly with a circulation of 60,000. All these papers have black editors who, while they may operate without direct interference from their employers, know well the limits of free expression in South Africa. Each of them has spent time in jail. In fact, the claim so often heard that South Africa enjoys "the freest press in Africa" could never have applied to anything but the white press. Many small, independent papers have been banned or hounded out of existence. Those black community papers that survive are constantly seeing their editions banned, their offices burned down, their reporters and editors attacked and jailed. Four major papers, all of them predecessors of the *Sowetan,* were banned, each time costing the Argus Company large sums that it does not plan to pay again— with the result that the *Sowetan* is, in the words of its editor, "quite muffled."

The initial impression gained from a big-city newsstand in South Africa—of a rich variety of voices, the basic condition for a healthy press—is, therefore, largely an illusion. Only a relatively narrow band of opinion is allowed to publish. Still, the black papers are notably fiercer in their opposition to the government than any of the white papers. Black papers are understaffed, however, and lack the resources to do much beyond covering local news. Moreover, the white papers often compete for black readers by publishing so-called extra editions, for black readers. Traditionally, extra editions have been strong on sports, sex, crime, the sensational, and the supernat-

ural, and have been scorned by black spokesmen for their con-
descension.

The *Star* Africa edition has some of the quality of a traditional
extra. It often replaces the first business page of the white edition
with a page of letters from black readers, news from the rest of
Africa, and a medical advice column directed at blacks. And its
sports section, which replaces news of rugby, a predominantly
white sport, with news of soccer, a predominantly black sport,
has a distinctly downmarket tone. But the *Star* Africa edition
distinguishes itself from the white editions primarily by its news
selection. News from the black townships and the bantustans is
given more space and prominence than news that is mainly of
interest to whites. On June 4, 1986, to pick a day at random,
page-one stories in the white edition about the failure of an
insurance company and charges that the national rugby side had
received secret payments for a match became, in the Africa
edition, a story about blacks defying police restrictions on the
funeral of an unrest victim and a story about four black admin-
istrators resigning under pressure from a government-sponsored
township council. Sometimes the same story will run under
different headlines in the different editions. Thus, when a black
woman won a house in a white suburb in a sweepstakes, causing
the authorities some consternation, the Africa edition of June 19
brusquely announced, "BLACK HAWKER WINS WHITE HOUSE,"
while the white edition went with the gentler "CONTEST WINNER
WILL RECEIVE NEW HOME IN DAVEYTON."

Sometimes the differences between editions seem even more
cosmetic. On June 3, both black and white editions ran page-one
photos to illustrate the onset of cold weather, the difference being
that the white edition used white subjects for its photo while the
Africa edition used blacks. Even such innocent fare can become
the occasion for sharp commentary, though. The white-edition
photo showed two teenage girls looking darling in ski sweaters,
ski caps, and wool gloves; the Africa edition photo showed a
group of men, women, and children who had lost their squatters'
shacks in police-directed vigilante attacks shivering around a fire
in the rain.

Separate editions reflect the separate realities that black and white South Africans inhabit. (And comparing exclusively-black papers with exclusively-white papers provides far starker reflections. Thus, the large advertisements for firearms in *Die Vaderland*—urging whites, who are already the most heavily-armed population per capita in the world, to protect their families with yet more Lugers and shotguns—become, in *City Press*, small ads for toy pistols that make "a big sound just like a real gun"—real guns being effectively illegal for blacks to own.) Separate editions also carry heavy loads of implied information about the colliding passions and the vastly different priorities of oppressor and oppressed. In the white editions, the deaths of white soldiers are mourned and the rise of a far-right white political movement is carefully monitored. The Africa edition ignores the white far right—while reporting extensively on factional splits within the black resistance—and turns its attention to white soldiers only when they attack a black funeral. The white editions don't record the funeral, much less the attack, and most white *Star* readers don't know even the foremost figures or the basic issues in the debates that divide the black resistance. Papers like the *Star* are widely criticized for deepening the gulfs of apartheid with separate editions instead of trying to bridge them. But, while Rex Gibson, sensitive to this criticism, was trying to reduce the differences between his black and white editions, and declaring his intention of eventually unifying them altogether—spurning the commercial considerations that launched the Africa edition in the first place—reporters on the Africa edition objected to the idea. Most of the *Star*'s black reporters are assigned to the Africa edition (only one white reporter works there) and most of them believe that a unified paper will simply be a white paper again.

For all their crusading against apartheid, the white opposition newspapers are regularly excoriated by black South Africans. Bishop (now Archbishop) Desmond Tutu, in a speech to newspaper editors and publishers in Vienna in May, 1986, after dismissing the SABC as "a lickspittle sycophant of the government," and the Afrikaans papers as "propaganda agents for the government," and the *Citizen* as "the shameless spawn of the Info Scandal," accused the English-language papers of having "sold their souls in exchange for immediate realizable advantages, mainly financial ones, which go hand in glove with popularity in the white community." The English-language press, according to Tutu, had failed in its historic mission by catering to white fears and prejudices, and failing to convey to the papers' white readers the reality of black experience. "They do not in their heart of hearts appear to believe that the present dispensation is on the skids, that change is going to happen and that when it does, there may have to be a day of reckoning when every institution and everybody will be judged and judged harshly about whether they advanced or hindered the liberation process." To Tutu, and to many other blacks, the opposition of the liberal press to the government has never gone far enough, never amounted to support for black liberation, to an unhedged demand for nonracial democracy—for, that is, one-person-one-vote in a unitary South Africa.

And it is not only blacks, or those clearly advocating the cause of black liberation, or the government, who take the English-language press to task for its role in the current crisis. Ken Owen, an influential conservative newspaper editor, in a recent essay flayed the *Star* for the meager coverage, in its white editions, of the fighting in the townships, contending that, "whether or not it was carrying out government wishes, the newspaper managed to deceive its readers about the extent and nature of the threat they faced."

Chapter 3

Gunfire and Jingles

I had lived in South Africa before, in 1980 and 1981, but things had changed enormously in the five years I had been away. On my first morning back, I went walking through the Johannesburg suburb where I had arranged to stay. The winter light was intensely pure and fresh, the earth richly red, the highveld sky heartbreakingly blue. It all brought back a flood of memories: the ineffable natural pleasures of southern Africa. Then I rounded a corner and saw, spray-painted in big black letters on a brick wall opposite a police station: VIVA UMKHONTO WE SIZWE! (Umkhonto we Sizwe is the military wing of the African National Congress, which has been outlawed in South Africa since 1960 and operates from underground.) For a moment, I just stared. I had never seen anything like this bold battle cry in a white suburb before. I glanced nervously toward the police station, which looked peaceful enough behind its barbed-wire fence. As I turned away, I caught the eye of a black man of about thirty who was standing in the sunshine reading, of all papers, the *Citizen*. He returned my nod, then said, with no visible irony, "Morning, *baas*."

On the whole, though, the white suburbs, tranquil in their insularity, seemed little changed. What had really changed were the townships. I had worked as a teacher in a "coloured" high school in Cape Town, had been through a three-month-long student boycott, and had seen the townships explode in major violence, so I thought I already knew something about resistance and conflict in black South Africa. But I was completely unprepared for the level of violence, the rage, the radicalization I found in 1986. The lives of millions of ordinary black people had been turned upside down by the fighting that began in September, 1984. Blacks in general seemed to be in an apocalyptic frame of mind. The police had always been an occupying force in the townships, but now the Army itself was heavily deployed there. In fact, the only whites one saw in the townships were the security forces: grim young soldiers in combat gear riding through the coal smoke, automatic rifles at the ready, in evil-looking armored vehicles known as Casspirs, Buffels, or Hippos. It was hard to imagine a white teacher in a black school now. I had worked legally in Cape Town, but work permits for foreigners had become virtually unobtainable—particularly for journalists. This time, I was in the country on a tourist visa.

On my first afternoon back, I went to see the sister of a friend who had left South Africa years before. She lives in Alexandra, an old black township northeast of Johannesburg, but she refused to let me visit her there. Instead, we met in an industrial area on the edge of the township, and there sat talking in my car. Across the road was a cluster of new brick buildings—a police barracks—from which government jeeps and trucks came and went constantly, ferrying groups of black men, some of them in uniform. These were policemen who had been driven from their homes in Alexandra. They kept looking in our direction, which made me uneasy, but my companion dismissed them with a contemptuous gesture. "We call them green beans, because of their green uniforms," she said. "We don't worry about *them* anymore."

My friend's sister was fifty years old, rail-thin, with a nice smile but a permanently pained expression. Whenever the conversation strayed from news of her brother, every scrap of which she gratefully devoured, she would sigh and say, "It is very, very bad here." Her contempt for the police did not seem to extend to the Army, which was heavily deployed in Alexandra. "It is just so dangerous now. I can't tell you. It is like a war," she said, and then, dropping her voice to a whisper, confided that she did not mind having the troops in Alexandra, because they made it easier for her to get to her job as a secretary. The Army was apparently taking a "hearts-and-minds" approach to the residents of Alexandra (as opposed to the rifles-and-rifle-butts approach they were using in KwaNdebele). My friend's sister did not blame the comrades for the fighting, though; she blamed the government. "They have pressurized us for so long, this must just happen," she said. "Someday it will be better." In the meantime, she had decided to quit her job and leave the city. She had just bought a plot of land next to her mother's in the KaNgwane bantustan.

Her brother had fled the country in 1976. When I asked if she had any news for him, perhaps about his old friends, she shook her head. "Some of those who left with him have come back," she said. "They come underground. They have been trained. But many of those boys are now serving long prison sentences. And some of them are late. Yes, several of his good friends are now late. But I wouldn't like him to hear that, all alone there in America."

When it came time to part, I offered her a lift home, but she refused it, insisting that it was too dangerous for me in the township—or, alternatively, that the fighting had played havoc with her housekeeping. "My furniture, which is quite nice, gets completely covered with dust," she said. "If you could see it, you wouldn't believe it." I later discovered that just having me drop her off could also have been dangerous for *her*. Someone might have seen me, a strange white man, rumors might have started and got twisted until people decided that someone from "the system" had been there, and her house could have ended up being firebombed. When we parted, she urged me repeatedly to drive quickly out of the area, stopping for no one, because hundreds of cars had been hijacked in and around Alexandra in the previous weeks.

As it happened, I went into Alexandra a few days later, es-

corted by a young activist named Sipho—a slick, vague kid
wearing a three-piece suit. We went in my rental car, a canary-
yellow VW CitiGolf. Sipho made me stop at the edge of the
township. He wanted to drive. I was agreeable. Sipho told me to
have some identification out, in my hand, ready to show to
anyone who managed to stop us. I took out my driver's license.
Sipho headed off into a blinding low sun, driving like a maniac
through the wide, rubble-strewn streets, screeching around cor-
ners, scattering people who shouted after us. Nobody managed
to stop the hurtling CitiGolf. We flew into a driveway, stashed
the car behind a house, and scurried inside.

Most of Alexandra is brick hovels or bleak flats, with no electricity or indoor plumbing, but the house we entered was what is
called in South Africa "black middle-class." The living room was
carpeted, modern, with big brass Buddhas on the mantel. The
lady of the house stared at me, as did her children—I couldn't
tell what their relation to Sipho was—but they seemed to grasp
immediately, and to accept, that I was a foreign journalist, there
to interview residents.

It was not an easy afternoon. An assortment of people—other
comrades, little kids, matrons from the neighborhood—joined us
for tea, but the atmosphere, to my mind, was excruciatingly
tense. Everyone in the room froze each time a vehicle passed,
barely breathing until young sentries peeking through the heavy
curtains hissed that the street was clear. Conversation would
resume—but my concentration would be shot. The others were
used to this level of fear; I was not.

There had been a great deal of fighting in Alexandra. Residents claimed that eighty people had been killed by the security
forces since the beginning of the year; the police figure was
thirty. The fighting was a gross mismatch: while the comrades
threw stones and half-bricks, and used homemade catapults to
launch crude missiles made out of nuts and bolts and old spark-
plugs, the security forces fired shotguns, tear gas, and high-
powered rifles from inside their armored vehicles. The residents
chuckled lightly, though, about the shortage of soft-drink bottles
in the township—they had all gone for Molotov cocktails, known

as "petrol bombs"—and about what they called "the clothes line." This was the name for a trap favored by the comrades: a strand of barbed wire strung across a road at the height of a soldier standing in the top of a Hippo.

I asked about the "people's courts" that were reported to be flourishing in Alexandra. The government and the white press regularly deplored them as kangaroo courts, meting out savage, arbitrary justice, but I heard nothing but praise for them from the residents of Alexandra. They were curbing public drunkenness and petty criminality, were fair in their sentencing, and always gave those accused a chance to defend themselves. A thief might be sentenced to clean up an empty lot, or water the grass in one of the many small parks that the comrades had built around the townships. A young miscreant might be forbidden to wear the T-shirt of the local youth organization—a stinging punishment in a community where the youth organization has become the local incarnation of the freedom struggle, and its uniform is its T-shirt—or obliged, perhaps, to attend political-education classes run by the comrades to counter the "poison education" received in government schools.

Everybody talked about the green beans, and about the "balaclava men"—gangs of masked police and vigilantes who had been going on murderous rampages through the township. People often interrupted one another to ask exactly which person at which address had met some gruesome fate, then shook their heads and clucked their tongues over the answers. Several people complained about the press coverage of the fighting. "They show nothing. People who are not here have no idea what is happening here," said a young man wearing a T-shirt emblazoned with the logo of the Congress of South African Students, a national organization of black high school students that was outlawed in 1985.

The most interesting person I talked with that day was a chubby, pretty, soft-spoken woman named Ruth. She was a secretary in her forties and she spoke plainly, without rhetoric. Her teen-age son had been jailed without charges for three months, she told me. For the first month, she had not known where he was, or even whether he was alive: many mothers were simply informed by the authorities that their children were dead and already buried; others never heard. "When he was released, there was something wrong with his heart," she told me. "The police struck him too many times. The doctor told me he must not get excited. But how can you tell a seventeen-year-old boy that he must not get excited? Especially with all that is happening to us now." Ruth's son was on the run. She saw him occasionally, when he came home for a change of clothes, and friends of his who were also running sometimes slept at her house. But the police came regularly, bursting in, hoping to find her son, and seizing any other comrades they found there. "I have not slept properly for a year or more," Ruth said, and I believed her. Like my friend's sister, she wore an expression of permanent pain and was given to quietly apocalyptic remarks. Several times that afternoon, she murmured, to no one in particular, "I wish the whole world would just blow up."

Then people started talking about a woman from the neighborhood who had been necklaced. The woman had been an *impimpi*, a police informer. She had been warned twice to stop. Finally, a wounded comrade was thrown by the police into a Hippo and found her sitting inside. "Usually, informers may sit inside the Hippos, identifying houses, and who is an activist among those the police have captured," someone explained to me. "But they normally wear masks, and they never speak when someone from the community might hear them—they point. But this woman just sat there quite calmly, with no mask, and said, 'Hello, comrade.' " People whistled and clucked their tongues. "Soon after that, they caught her and burned her. This was in Ninth Street."

Ruth turned to me and said, very slowly, emphasizing every word, "I think the necklace is a good thing." Her eyes were full of strange, sad anger. She went on, "It makes the people think twice before they will collaborate, even if they have no job and the system offers them money to inform. We are unarmed. They are armed. We must take and use the little weapons we have.

Informers have been the system's greatest weapon for a very long time. Finally, now, we are stopping them."

For very different reasons in vastly different places, the necklace was an inescapable—and incendiary—topic wherever one went in South Africa. A few nights after my visit to Alexandra, I was having dinner with a group of white academics. One of my companions, a courtly old geophysicist with a piercing voice, had been amusing the table with stories featuring himself as a young, lumbering, cowardly Afrikaner forever being threatened by ruffians: mistaken for Richard Widmark by a knife-wielding drunk at a carnival; hiding under the bed in a Boston rooming house while a pretty neighbor's gangster boyfriend pounded on the door; apologizing to derelicts whom he had somehow insulted on a beach in Sydney.

Conversation turned, inexorably, to the necklace. The geophysicist offered the opinion that whites who thought that necklacing proved that blacks were savages were making unwarranted racial generalizations. The act itself was savage, barbaric, bestial, certainly, but blacks other than the perpetrators should not be blamed for it. His remarks did not meet with much approbation—it was a more liberal, sophisticated group than that. Someone pointed out that the French Resistance during the Second World War routinely executed those suspected of collaborating with the Germans, often with less evidence, it seemed, than blacks had against their neighbors who were informers, and without the multiple warnings that were apparently common in the townships. Someone else suggested that the South African media made much more of the cruelty and horror of necklacing than it did of the cruelty and horror of soldiers shooting children in the back, when the latter was really a more horrifying sort of murder, if one wanted to rank murder by degrees, as the law did. The press coverage seemed to play to white fears of the black mob, while ignoring black fears of the police and Army.

The geophysicist listened in silence to these demurrals.

But then I described Ruth, and repeated her remarks, and he

blew up. He accused me of excusing Ruth's "barbarism, her savagery," because of a political program that *I* wanted to impose on South Africa. He compared Ruth to Adolf Hitler. He angrily brought up the fact that his mother had twice been "criminally assaulted by blacks," and when I did not respond, he thundered, "You don't care about my mother?!"

After dinner, I went for a drive to soothe my nerves. As I wandered through the wide, wet, well-lit streets, hearing on the radio that "Bushmanland and the Northern Cape will be cloudy and cold, with showers," I thought about how, as little as things might seem to have changed in white South Africa, there was in fact a constantly rising anxiety level that, in recent days, often focused on foreigners. White South Africans were afraid of black rebellion, but that fear was vague; they were much more clearly disturbed by their increasing international isolation.

The government press expressed the mood, which was a sort of paranoid mixture of entreaty and truculence, precisely with its ritual admissions that apartheid had all been a great mistake, followed by equally ritual rejections of any and all criticism coming from the morally bankrupt West, or from anywhere else in what *Beeld,* the Johannesburg morning daily, called "a venomous world." White South Africa could not hope to be understood: "The prejudice and hate are much too great." White attitudes toward the disinvestment issue—among both the government's supporters *and* its liberal, anti-apartheid opponents—verged on the hysterical. The same was true for the international cultural boycott: a recent article in the *Sunday Times,* a national opposition weekly, had presented a lengthy list of foreign artists who earned places on the "U.N.'s silly blacklist" by coming to South Africa *and then saw their careers take off*—as if visiting South Africa had somehow catapulted them to success.

The most poignant symptom I had seen was a campaign being mounted by the South African Tourism Board to try to combat all this rejection misery. The full-color double-page advertisements in the *Star* were almost painful to look at. The ads began, "QUICK. NAME SOMEONE YOU'D LIKE TO VISIT SOUTH AFRICA, FREE." It seemed the Tourism Board was giving away 150 round-trip air tickets to South Africa, and inviting *Star* readers to submit the names of overseas friends and family for a drawing. The winners would get the tickets, and their local sponsors would get the chance to "let them know South Africa is still a great place to visit." Under a long row of photographs in warm-toned, bureau-top frames, the ad made suggestions about the kind of people one might want to nominate: "The charming Joneses who were out from Birmingham four years ago"; "Your daughter's penfriend"; "The girl you met on the plane to Mauritius." Everyone in the photos was white; everyone being asked to respond to the ad was clearly white, too.

I drove on into Hillbrow, a seedy night-life district, where, on the main drag, black men bullfight the passing cars from both sides of the road, whipping white towels at drivers in frantic attempts to signal them into parking spaces over which, for a small fee, they will stand sentry. Hillbrow's high-rise apartments are being rapidly, illegally integrated—there are reportedly ten thousand black people already living in the area, a situation much-cited as evidence of how South African society is changing, even if certain laws (such as the Group Areas Act, which regulates racial segregation in housing) are not. This isn't the sort of change that necessarily thrills blacks, of course. Driving through Hillbrow on another night with a black reporter, I noticed him curling his lip at the crowds and bright lights and asked him why. "Capitalism," he said, with intense disgust. "Decadence."

A friend of mine says that, if one were to write a symphony about present-day South Africa, it would have to include both gunfire and commercial jingles, African war chants and Bruce Springsteen. And each of the movements would have to be composed, I think, in its own obtuse notation. When I arrived in Johannesburg, I was startled to find the same bumper sticker— "I ♡ Soweto"—on nearly every vehicle being driven by a black person. The distribution of the thing outdid that of any other fad item I had ever heard of. What was more, the sentiment it expressed seemed incomprehensible. Were people really ready to embrace—and in this utterly ersatz way—the ghetto where they were forced to live under apartheid? Everyone I asked about it agreed that it was quite a craze, but none of them could tell me what was behind it. Then, on my first visit to Soweto, I saw young boys hawking the stickers at every major intersection: thrusting them in the windows of taxis and vans, slapping at the sides of passing cars with thick stacks of them. Since every vehicle in sight already sported at least one "I ♡ Soweto" on its bumper, this made no sense whatsoever. I asked my companions, Soweto residents both, what gave. They squirmed, they grumbled. Finally, one of them said, "Somebody's really exploiting the situation. They're making a mint out of the people's fear."

I asked what that meant.

"It means people try to use those things to show that their car or truck is not a company car, not a white man's vehicle—that it belongs to a black person. They hope to avoid being attacked, or having their vehicle burned, that way."

This rude mix of hucksterism and terror, I realized, was a perfect metaphor for life in the townships in 1986. (I continued to ask white South Africans about the "I ♡ Soweto" stickers, just to see what they would say, but I never met one who knew why they were so popular.) Far-sighted black entrepreneurs actively embraced the revolution. A few days after my eye-opening on the bumper-sticker question, a Soweto liquor distributor took out a newspaper advertisement to salute "our fallen heroes"—those killed in protests—"who have sacrificed supremely to give birth to a people's education for a better and brighter future for all." And a Soweto car dealer donated a Ford Escort XR3 for the grand prize in a "People's Giant Raffle" being staged in Fun Valley, Soweto, by the Release Mandela Campaign.

Soweto itself, while undoubtedly ♡ed by many people—Jon Qwelane claims that he, for one, would live nowhere else, even if he were permitted to—has the same higgledy-piggledy, fear-edged, endlessly incongruous quality that the situation as a whole in South Africa has. It is the largest city in southern Africa, but it is also not a city at all. Amenities are few and furtive:

practically all the bars are illegal, located in private homes; there are three cinemas to serve the estimated two million residents; whenever possible, people do their shopping in Johannesburg, twenty miles away. Most of those who live in Soweto are poor, of course, but some are far poorer than others. There are vast "hostels" where migrant workers live in gulag conditions, strictly segregated from more permanent residents. There are crowded, filthy shantytowns stalked by disease, hunger, and evil-looking dogs. Only a stone's throw away (*the* measure of distance in the townships these days) from these hells-on-earth are modern ranch-style houses with sliding glass doors, indoor plumbing, and sports cars in the driveways—the houseproud, upmarket neighborhoods, known locally by mordant nicknames like Beverly Hills and Prestige Park, where the Tutus and the Mandelas live. Schools are numerous but pokey and rundown and, while I was around, they were usually vacant. The fields around them, like fields throughout the township, tended to be blackened, for grass fires were believed to help disperse tear gas.

The atmosphere in the Soweto streets could be deceptively peaceful, even somnolent, with donkey carts clopping down the long, monotonous rows of matchbox houses, small children pushing steel chair frames around in the dirt, women hanging laundry on backyard lines. . . . And then suddenly the air would electrify around a group of youths gathering stones to greet a delivery van or a Hippo or a "mellow yellow"—the absurd name blacks have given to the yellow police vans that, completely encased in shells of heavy steel mesh, patrol the townships. Like so many other South African townships, Soweto is both a bedroom community and a war zone. At night, the violence escalates wildly, with rape, robbery, and nonpolitical murder keeping pace easily with the more era-specific mayhem of firebombings, assassinations, police shootings, and raids on the homes of activists.

Beyond the basic outlines of the fighting—the black resistance against the apartheid state—the war raging in the townships could seem, especially to an outsider, quite chaotic. The security forces employed black vigilantes—the balaclava gangs—to attack their opponents; the resistance groups frequently fought among themselves. And the carnage had been terrible. As of June, 1986, at least two thousand people had died and untold thousands had been maimed or wounded in political violence since the beginning of the uprising in September, 1984.

If there was a coordinated resistance strategy, it was concentrated on the destruction of the community council system, created by the state to place local township administration in politically reliable black hands, and on the establishment of alternative bodies—civic associations, street committees, "people's courts." How much of all this resistance activity was in response to the calls by African National Congress leaders for "people's war," and how much, if any, was being directly coordinated by ANC operatives, was a point of unending debate. The leading aboveground resistance organization, the United Democratic Front—a multiracial alliance, founded in 1983, of approximately seven hundred organizations with nearly two million members— is clearly aligned with the ANC's goals, and the state had charged a number of UDF leaders with treason for "furthering the aims" of the ANC. (A common, and fiercely ironic, accusation in the "people's courts" in the townships was "furthering the aims" of the police.) Whatever its exact size and role may be, the underground is a powerful presence, and the periodic bombings and other "armed propaganda" it produces are definitely not the full extent of its involvement in resistance. It is, above all, this unknown quantity that makes the true state of the South African revolution so difficult to describe. Even the few journalists who may know anything about the underground cannot write what they know.

What one can say with certainty is that apartheid, for all the rumors of its death, lives on most rudely. The African majority is still denied, on the basis of race, the vote. People classified "coloured" or Indian have a token franchise, but the government is really accountable only to the white minority. Not only does racial segregation in housing and education and politics remain the law—the Minister of Home Affairs recently assured the whites-only Parliament that the system of racial classification is "behind lock and key," and will never be abandoned—but the profound inequities that flow inevitably from such a system remain as grotesque as ever. Thus, while whites enjoy a surplus of housing in the areas set aside for their exclusive use, blacks, forced to live in the townships, suffer from a profound shortage. A recent study found that seven and a half million urban Africans compete for less than half a million "relatively small housing units"; in the townships near Uitenhage, in the eastern Cape, the study found up to forty-two people living in a two-bedroom house. Health care, education, and the other social services are similarly maldistributed. Even in the courts, which are considered a bastion of independence from the government, virtually all of the magistrates and judges are white, and the racial disparities in sentencing are staggering. A white policeman is fined the equivalent of twelve dollars for the unprovoked murder of a "coloured" man in Johannesburg, and two white soldiers are fined the equivalent of twenty dollars for roasting an African man over a fire and raping his wife. Meanwhile, a black woman found in possession of a book, published by Penguin, that is alleged to further the aims of the ANC is sentenced to eighteen months in jail.

One more thing that can be said with certainty about this chaotic time in South Africa is that it is continually producing the most bizarre contrasts and anomalies. In the suburb where I was staying, a free neighborhood newspaper appeared on the porch each week. Called the *Northeastern Tribune,* it consisted mostly of advertising, with front-page stories carrying headlines like "DOG LICENCE CRACKDOWN." A typical front-page photograph showed a top Boy Scout saluting. The paper was what is known as a "knock-and-drop." The number of knock-and-drops in South Africa has grown wildly in the last few years, as advertisers have found them to be effective marketing vehicles. In 1985, Ameen Akhalwaya, a South African journalist of Indian descent, and a former Nieman fellow at Harvard, started up a knock-and-drop called *The Indicator* in the Indian township of Lenasia, near Soweto. *The Indicator* looks much like the *Northeastern Tribune*: same tabloid format, lots of local advertising. But Akhalwaya's idea in founding a knock-and-drop was less to provide a vehicle for advertisers than it was to see if he could, by publishing in a medium that is as yet exempt from normal newspaper censorship, avoid the official assaults that have closed all previous black-owned newspapers in South Africa. A typical lead story in *The Indicator* might be the exposure of a police dirty-tricks campaign—the distribution of phony pamphlets under a UDF letterhead, say—or the defiant statements of political detainees upon their release from jail. A photograph in the first issue I saw showed, very graphically, the multiple wounds of a police torture victim. So far, *The Indicator* has been able to publish unhindered, the calls to revolution by Winnie Mandela alongside the ads for Sleeky Boutique. Such are the tactics that the resistance and journalists—and the two are not always distinguishable—have been compelled to employ.

Chapter 4

The Ghetto

When I met Ron Anderson, the editor of the daily *Star,* and told him that I would like to spend some time with his black reporters, he did not react well. He grumbled about bad experiences the paper had recently had with foreign reporters taking "cheap shots" at the practice of publishing separate editions. "Why should we hang our chins out there again?" he asked. Anderson, an older man, was wearing a short-sleeved white shirt, a brush mustache, and a worried expression. I tried to assure him that I had not come ten thousand miles to take a cheap shot, but he seemed unconvinced. He said that it was definitely too dangerous for me to accompany his reporters out in the field. He would have to think about the idea of my being around the newsroom at all, and see what Rex Gibson said.

On my way out, feeling discouraged, I saw Phil Mtimkulu, the news editor of the Africa edition, and Jon Qwelane coming across the newsroom. Mtimkulu had been my initial contact at the *Star,* and had taken me to Anderson, and he could see that I had got no joy there. I had never met Qwelane, but I recognized him from a photograph that runs with one of his weekend columns. I stopped and introduced myself. Mtimkulu moved on.

"What do you want?" Qwelane asked.

I took a deep breath and explained what I wanted to do. Qwelane heard me out, watching me closely, and said nothing for at least a minute after I finished. He just kept staring thoughtfully into my eyes. Finally, he said, in a raspy, smoker's voice, "We go to Tembisa in an hour. We've got a witness to a shooting there. You can come along if you like."

I was stunned. Tembisa, a black township in the East Rand, had been racked with violence. "Wouldn't it be dangerous?"

"I can't guarantee your safety. Are you coming?"

I guessed I was.

"Where are you staying?"

I told him.

"Go there. We'll pick you up in an hour."

"Are you sure you can find it?"

Qwelane chuckled. "It's in a white area," he said. "It has an address. We can find it."

That first trip with Qwelane to Tembisa never happened—our witness to a shooting disappeared. But I took my cue from him that first afternoon and never again sought the permission of management to travel with the *Star* reporters. I simply turned up at the newsroom each day, got to know the people I wanted to know, and the people who didn't know me soon began to assume I worked there. Young white sub-editors would pass the desk where I sat answering phones ("Newsroom") and writing up the day's events and cheerfully commiserate, "On nights this week? Better than courts, at least."

The *Star* newsroom is a U-shaped acre of video terminals. The dominant decorative mode is molded plastic and institutional shades of beige. The windows look across busy streets at other third-floor office windows. The senior editors' private offices line the north wall, where they catch the afternoon sun before it disappears behind the modernist bulk of the Johannesburg Stock Exchange. The section of the newsroom set aside for the staff of the *Sunday Star* extends the U on one side, and thus seems semi-autonomous, and the sports department is marked off by a few low temporary partitions, but otherwise the vast room feels undifferentiated—at least at night, when it's all but deserted. The only memorable bit of décor is a series of huge black-and-white photographs that run from floor to ceiling. One of these, looming behind the desk of the editor of the women's page, shows a burning fuel-storage tank. Another, in the foyer by the elevators, shows a smiling black soldier dancing, with his rifle held over his head. To anyone familiar with the recent history of southern Africa, the fuel-storage tank is plainly SASOL One, the South African oil-from-coal plant, after the devastating 1980 bombing by African National Congress guerrillas. And the soldier, just as plainly, is from FRELIMO; he is celebrating the liberation of Mozambique from Portuguese rule, in 1975; the gun he is waving is a Soviet-made AK-47. I asked around, but no one at the *Star* seemed to know who was responsible for these giant images of armed revolution and black liberation on the walls of the newsroom. People had ceased to notice them.

During working hours, the *Star* newsroom teems. Reporters, photographers, editors hurry around, the rows of terminals are manned, and the impersonal-looking office becomes a dense mini-society of concentric and interlocking communities. I spent most of my time there in what Qwelane calls "the ghetto"—that corner of the newsroom, hard by the sports department, where the black reporters work. While I was around, there were six black reporters working out of the newsroom, plus Phil Mtim-kulu, the one black editor at the *Star*. Three of the six—Montshiwa Moroke, Mike Tissong and Mudini Maivha—worked for Phil on the Africa edition. Maud Motanyane, the only woman in the group, was assigned to the main edition. Mike Siluma shared the labor beat with a white reporter. And Qwelane, of course, was on the Sunday paper. He was never to be found in the distant *Sunday Star* wing of the newsroom, though, and he claimed not even to know which desk there was supposed to be his. The phone number he gave to sources rang only in the ghetto, and he made do with terminals that officially belonged to others. It was said that Ron Anderson was determined to break up the newsroom ghetto, and would soon be taking measures toward that end. But the more time I spent with the *Star*'s black reporters, the less I thought of the editor's chances of success. Together with the *Star*'s two black photographers, Herbert Mabuza and Alf Kumalo, they were a very close group, intricately and passionately bound to one another by all the danger, confusion, dedication, and rage they shared.

Chapter 5

In Katlehong

The first time I accompanied one of the *Star*'s reporters out on assignment was on a Saturday morning in early June. It had been a bloody week—half a dozen different political funerals were scheduled that day in half a dozen different townships near Johannesburg. Because the black reporters' stories would probably be appearing in the *Sunday Star*, whose township coverage was Qwelane's responsibility, Qwelane was coordinating their assignments that morning. He was in high gear before anyone left the newsroom—flashing between terminals to touch up stories that were going in that day's paper, taking nonstop phone calls about the shifting times, venues, and prospects for the day's ceremonies, improvising a schedule for maximum coverage by the available reporters and photographers. At one point, scanning a story in that morning's paper, Qwelane whirled and peered at a poster on the newsroom wall—it was the *Star*'s street poster for the day: "COURT LIFTING BAN ON UDF MEETINGS"—and he frowned. "That poster's misleading," he said. But it was too late to do anything about it. "The newsboys have probably torn them all down and burnt them, anyway," Qwelane said. It was a cold morning and I, too, had noticed, on my way into town, young newspaper vendors huddled next to trash-can fires.

Qwelane decided that the potential for violence at the Soweto service he would be covering was becoming unacceptably high and, in a rushed, serious tone that did not invite argument, suggested that I go with Mudini Maivha to the East Rand.

We took the freeway southeast. As the skyscrapers of downtown Johannesburg fell behind, I asked Maivha about his background. "I am a migrant laborer," he said. "My wife is in the northern Transvaal. I only see her and our daughter, who is two years old, on holidays." Maivha, twenty-seven, rumpled and earnest and lithe, was wearing thin blue socks, shiny black shoes, slacks several inches too short, and a new beige "lumberjacket." Long-faced and narrow-eyed, he had a manner, a peculiarly African combination of awkwardness and dash, of deep-voiced seriousness and unreadable mirth, that reminded me of ex-guerrillas I had met in Zimbabwe. Maivha is actually not the sort of person who comes first to mind when one thinks of the millions of migrant laborers in South Africa—very few of whom have cars and drivers put at their disposal at work—but his home in Soweto, as I later saw, was as modest as any poor black worker's. It was a tiny, cement-floored room in a garage that had been divided into three separate apartments. The curtains were newspapers, the toilet was across the yard. Somehow Maivha shared the room. His roommate, a nineteen-year-old boy who also came from the north, wanted to go to art school to study painting. Maivha showed me two of his paintings. They were cheap, vivid oils on particle board. One showed a burning landscape, the other an anguished African face.

Unwisely, considering that we were on our way into townships known for their volatility with a driver already grumbling about "unrest," I asked Maivha about close calls he had had as a reporter. He shrugged. "I once wrote a story about a group called the Society for Young Africa, and I mentioned in it that they were allegedly involved in an attack on a foundation official who had refused them access to some facility. I called the group for comment, but they wouldn't comment. I didn't think any more about it. Then, a few months later, I went to cover one of their meetings. Their leader saw me, and he told the members that I should be killed. He said, 'He has been writing shit about us.' So about two hundred of them attacked me. They knocked me down and I covered my head, but they just came at me, *whack whack whack*." Maivha threw his fingers down so that the knuckles made a sharp, slapping noise. He shook his head sadly. "I thought I was going to die. But their leader eventually got a fright and called them off. I just got out of there, and went straight to the hospital. I was quite badly beaten, but I had only one serious injury—a gash in the thigh."

We were off the freeway now, with Maivha directing the driver through a patchwork of small farms and white suburbs. "Funerals can be quite tricky, too," he mused. "Once, we were driving along in a funeral procession, going very slowly, when the crowd suddenly decided to lift up the car. It was one of these Toyotas, and they simply lifted it up off its wheels. There were people shouting that they should turn it over and burn it, despite the fact that there were four old ladies in the back seat. Four old ladies *from the community*. They weren't planning to let us get out, either."

"What happened?"

"I just told them they were acting irrationally. I asked them to tell me about their problems with the press. I said, 'I'm here to represent the public that cannot be here.' Fortunately, they accepted that. The situation has changed drastically since that time, though. The same line wouldn't work now. The cooperation we journalists used to enjoy has been eroded."

The road we were traveling turned to dirt. Then we were in Katlehong or Thokoza or Vosloorus: all three townships are in the same part of the East Rand, and to an unpracticed eye they are identical—rutted dirt roads, endless rows of matchbox houses, sad little schools and churches, big, dusty bus depots, suspicious people peering into a strange car. Maivha, who speaks nine languages (his mother tongue is Venda), asked for directions in Zulu and Sotho and Tsonga. He is accomplished in the art of approaching strangers, donning an air of such meekness and respect that no one can believe for long that he's a cop. At one place, we saw a group of teen-age boys flee into the middle distance, stop, call to friends, pick up rocks, and start advancing carefully back toward the car. Maivha got out and walked toward the boys. He clasped his hands in front of him and half crouched, bowing and murmuring and generally conveying an impression so unthreatening that five minutes later he had four teenagers crammed in the back seat with me, giving directions in Zulu to the funeral we wanted to cover.

The comrades were in uniform: red-and-yellow T-shirts silk-screened with the logo of the United Democratic Front, the slogan "June 16, South African Youth Day," and a well-known photograph of thirteen-year-old Hector Petersen—the first casualty of the 1976 uprising, killed by a police bullet—lying limp in the arms of a distraught older boy. Two of the comrades wore grubby bandanas; I remembered hearing that a bandana soaked in water or, better yet, lemon juice offered, when pulled over the face, a degree of protection against tear gas. (Reporters sometimes wore them, too.) The comrades directed us through the township streets, pointing out what Maivha explained were the houses of "activists, collaborators, informers." As we passed a burned-out, collapsed house, Maivha translated: "An activist lived there. The system says the house was petrol-bombed. But it was grenades, given to vigilantes by the cops. Petrol bombs don't blow two walls down."

We eventually found the house of a bereaved family. A tent had been set up in the yard, but the only people around were a few old women. They were cooking cornmeal in huge cast-iron pots over open fires—food for the mourners when they returned from the graveyard. Large metal tubs full of water were ranged around the yard. These were for the traditional washing of hands after the burial—still practiced, though graves are now dug by machines. The water could also be used, Maivha explained, for washing tear gas from one's eyes. The old women told the comrades where the funeral service was being held. We drove there.

It was a relatively prosperous-looking Catholic church, standing inside a compound wtih a high brick wall. The church was filled with well-dressed mourners. Three flower-covered coffins stood in front of the altar, one of them a child's. The mood was peaceful, muted, religious—not political. The service alternated brief eulogies, delivered in Sotho, with hymns. There were a number of comrades in the compound but few inside the church. Maivha and I sat in a rear pew, but my presence seemed to disrupt the service—people craned around to see the *umlungu*, rustling and muttering and peering—so we didn't stay long. Back out in the compound, Maivha went to work: he introduced himself to a group of church elders who were greeting mourners, politely questioned them about the deceased, and scribbled their answers in a battered little notebook.

The comrades—six or seven of them—began to gather around. Their leader, a short muscular man in his late twenties, took over the interview from the churchmen. The other comrades seemed mostly interested in me. I asked a couple of them questions, and got monosyllabic answers. Most of them just stared. They were a scary, uninspiring group—quite unlike some of the articulate, idealistic fighters I had met in Alexandra and elsewhere. The youngest of them was probably twelve, and they all bore an appalling number of scars on their faces and heads. The most disconcerting thing about them, though, was their eyes, which were absolutely expressionless. I wondered how many of them had been tortured. I wondered how many of them had participated in a necklacing. I wondered how long it had been since they were last in school—many black schools had been empty for two years, because of boycotts. And I wondered how well these kids understood the democratic ideas for which they were ostensibly fighting. The level of absolute intolerance within the resistance was reported to be rising as brutalized youths—what educated activists called "lumpen elements"—asserted themselves in the ever more violent atmosphere. These days, simply expressing a difference of opinion over tactics—asking at a community meeting whether, say, a boycott should not be called for two days instead of three—could, it was said, gain the intrepid questioner, even if he was a respected member of the community, a public threat of necklacing. These kids lived in a world of guns, bombs, terror, pain, death, and funerals. Maivha told me that they often wrapped old inner tubes around themselves, or wore double layers of clothes, to help ward off birdshot, rubber bullets, and sjamboks. My curiosity about their experience, their politics, my tentative questions, plainly failed to register among such primal considerations. Only my race, my strangeness, seemed to interest them.

Maivha did much better, naturally. As we left the funeral, he told me what he had learned. The dead were a murdered trade unionist, his brother (also murdered), and a child who had been hit by a car. The church elders had supplied him with names, ages, and details of the deaths. "But this was not really what you could call a political funeral," Maivha said. "After the unionist was killed, the comrades suspected his brother of the murder, so they killed him. And now the two brothers are being buried together." He shook his head. "The comrade said the child's death was political, because it is apartheid that makes the township roads unsafe." After a minute, Maivha sighed, and said, " 'Comrades' has become a very loosely used term. You often can't tell who is being referred to."

Using directions provided by the priest, we eventually reached another house with a funeral tent, water tubs, and old women cooking cornmeal. There we picked up two smartly dressed young women, who directed us to a Methodist church in Katlehong. The funeral at the Methodist church was for Margaret Komane, thirty-one, burned to death in a firebombing. This promised to be a political funeral—a young man had confessed, at a press conference held by the UDF, to being paid by the police to firebomb activists' houses, including the one in which Margaret Komane died. (He had confessed to other firebombings, too, including one in which an infant was killed; after the press conference, he was arrested by the police.)

The church was a barnlike old building, with a roof of corrugated metal. We decided to enter by the side door, near the altar, so that if people wanted to stare at me they wouldn't have to turn around. People did stare—the church was jammed with at least six hundred people, every one of whom seemed to turn and watch me closely as we squeezed into a pew near the side door. And the atmosphere was definitely political. Three young comrades were up in front of the altar trading a microphone back and forth and shouting, in a rather mesmerized way, revolutionary slogans, of which I could only catch occasional words: "vigilantes" and "the system" and "informers" and "UDF" and "ANC" and "SACP" (South African Communist Party) and "SADF" (South African Defence Force—the Army). Maivha, taking the room's emotional temperature and finding it dangerously high, quickly left the pew and approached the altar. He beckoned to an older man who was sitting in front of the altar, and drew him aside. I noticed that the walls of the church were plastered everywhere, even behind the altar, with red-and-yellow UDF posters: "UNBAN THE ANC." Piled high on the wooden coffin at the foot of the altar were shaggy-headed white chrysanthemums, tied with a lavender ribbon.

Maivha came back from the altar, and the man he had talked to took the microphone and began speaking in Zulu. To my dismay, he pointed a finger at me. The gathering's attention focused on me more intensely than ever. The only words of the speaker's message that I understood were "the system"—a dread phrase under the circumstances. I looked at Maivha, who whispered, "He is saying, 'It makes us very uncomfortable when we see a white man in a situation like this. We assume he is a representative of the system. But these people are journalists. They are not the enemy.' " Maivha gave me a wan smile. I thought of his words earlier about the "cooperation" that journalists *no longer* enjoyed. We turned our attention back to the altar. The crowd seemed to grow slightly less interested in us, and for that I was grateful.

But the seats we had taken were in the middle of a group of about two hundred comrades, many of whom continued to watch me suspiciously. A short, imposing man in purple clerical robes took the microphone. This was Simeon Nkoane, the Anglican Bishop Suffragan for Johannesburg East, and his sermon, in Zulu, seemed to enthrall much of the crowd. The comrades interrupted him every few minutes, though, with chants. Someone would shout, "Viva ANC!" or "Viva UDF!" and the others would answer, "Viva!"—thrusting fists into the air as they

roared. Some of those near us made it clear that they wanted us
to cheer along with them, so we too raised our fists and yelled,
"Viva!" Since I couldn't follow Bishop Nkoane's speech, Maivha
summarized it for me: "He says they must not burn informers.
They must convert them, because informers have useful information about the system."

The comrades tossed up another shout, I joined in on the
"Viva!"—and suddenly the comrades around us were laughing. I
looked at Maivha, who stared at me with a shocked expression.
After a minute, he whispered, "Nkoane says, 'Don't burn them.'
A comrade shouts, 'No, burn them!' And you say, 'Viva!' "

Bishop Nkoane, a passionate speaker but also an impressively
composed man, did not visibly react to the comrades' (or my)
chants. And the comrades did not seem to object to the religious
tenor of his message. (One of the few words in his sermon that I
understood was *"nkulunkulu"*—Zulu for "God"—a beautiful
word, which the Bishop used over and over, turning it into a
strangely intimate, rapturous refrain.) It seemed clear that, despite the rising tide of intolerance, the political economy of the
resistance could still accommodate the Bishop's and the comrades' separate perspectives. As the church service ended, the
whole crowd rose and sang, in Xhosa, "Nkosi Sikelel iAfrika"
("God Bless Africa"), the majestic Pan-African anthem of the
liberation struggle.

Maivha checked his watch as we hurried from the church. He
had a deadline coming up; he needed to file. The pastor's house,
next door, had a phone, we were told, so we ducked in there.
While Maivha phoned the newsroom, I watched a crowd gather
in the road outside for the march to the cemetery. There were
hundreds and hundreds of people—even more than had been
inside the church. The comrades began doing the *toyi-toyi*—a
dance that is scarcely more than rhythmic jogging in place but
when done in unison by hundreds of youths chanting war poems
has been known to cause soldiers of the South African Army to
panic, and fire indiscriminately. Margaret Komane's flower-
covered coffin appeared, borne on the shoulders of comrades

wearing berets. The crowd's singing began to fill the pastor's house with a compelling roar. Maivha crouched behind a sofa, trying to hear his call go through. But no one was answering in the newsroom. He finally hung up, looking perturbed. He couldn't wait until after the graveside rites to file, he said—that would be too late. We would have to rush back to the office now.

The crowd was setting off as we emerged. Its numbers would grow all the way to the graveyard, Maivha said. We found our car—the driver, not wanting to be associated with a suspicious vehicle, was not inside it, but materialized when he saw us—and headed for the highway. As we left Katlehong, Maivha pointed out two yellow police vans driving toward the cemetery on a road that ran parallel to the route of the funeral procession. He also pointed out more tubs of water set alongside the road, "for the use of those who may soon be suffering from tear gas," and front gates left open, "for those who may be running from the cops." Then Maivha spotted, in the distance, a Hippo headed toward the cemetery. "SADF," he said. "There's going to be a confrontation, and not a single reporter to cover it. But I have to file."

Twenty minutes later we were in the newsroom. It was very quiet—a lazy Saturday afternoon. The only stories breaking that day were the township funerals. There was nobody in the ghetto, which was where Maivha had phoned—everyone was still out in the field. Maivha went to work at a terminal, writing his story. I wandered over to the far side of the newsroom, where four white reporters and a black janitor were watching professional wrestling on television. Two fat blond men in skintight skivvies were throwing each other around, drawing loud laughter from the gang at the *Star*. I was seriously disoriented. So this was the looking glass through which the black reporters darted back and forth every day.

The other black reporters began turning up, all hurrying to terminals and going straight to work. Montshiwa Moroke had been in the township of Brits covering the funeral of a woman—the wife of a trade unionist—who had been killed in a firebombing. When I asked how it had been, he said, "Very powerful." The township, I later learned, had been sealed off by police. Moroke had got through the roadblocks by posing as an assistant to the driver of a delivery van.

Phil Mtimkulu had covered the funeral of Diliza Matshoba, a field worker for the South African Council of Churches, who had been killed in a car accident (not murdered, as many rumors had it). When I asked how it had gone, Mtimkulu said, "Tutu did his thing. The foreign press was there. There were no incidents." Then he got down to writing. Newspapers around the world, including the *Star*, ran a photograph the next day of Bishop Tutu, tears streaming down his face, pleading with his fellow blacks to stop killing one another.

Qwelane rushed into the newsroom. When he saw me, he said, "My God, I am glad I didn't let you go with me. There were bullets flying *everywhere*. It was a miracle no one was hit." He went to work. Within a few minutes, he had finished his piece and begun circulating among the desks of the other reporters. In the battle for space in the *Sunday Star*, Qwelane would end up having to combine most of the copy on the funerals into a single piece, led by his story, and then see that piece printed only in the Africa edition, with just a short version of Phil Mtimkulu's piece on the Matshoba funeral making it into the main edition. It seemed scant reward for a lot of dangerous work by a lot of dedicated people.

Chapter 6

A Strenuous
Profession

The role of the black journalist in South Africa has changed continually over the years. The country's first black writers, mission-educated intellectuals who lived in the late nineteenth and early twentieth centuries, typically became editors of African-language newspapers. After the destruction of tribally based resistance to white subjugation, these men were important spokesmen for blacks in general, and often became political leaders themselves. As literacy and the use of English grew, there emerged a white-owned English-language popular press directed at urban blacks, and with it a tradition of black reporters known for their street savvy, courageous reporting, and, in time, their literary style. The major figures of what came to be known as the Golden Era of black South African writing—Nat Nakasa, Can Themba, Bloke Modisane, Lewis Nkosi, Casey Motsisi, Ezekiel Mphahlele, men who flourished in the 1950s and early 1960s—were all working journalists. Writing in a vivid, Africanized English for *Drum* magazine and the *Golden City Post*, these reporters were not political figures as such, yet they won large followings with their investigations of official abuses and their sparkling evocations of life in the townships.

The community stature of the black reporter dwindled with

the passing of these legendary journalists—an appalling number
of whom died young from suicide or alcohol—and with a heavy
crackdown on dissent in the 1960s, which gutted all forms of
black expression. An ancillary view of the black reporter—one
that had been around for decades, existing side by side with the
reporter as inspired muckraker and modern bard—now came to
the fore. This was the reporter as low-status legman for the
papers in town, a slick character whose office was the shebeen (an
illegal tavern—it's a Gaelic word, brought to South Africa by the
Irish policemen who once worked in Cape Town), where he
drank, gambled, phoned in sports results for the extra edition,
and paid a few cents for news tips.

This stereotype, however, was permanently retired by the
events of 1976, when black townships throughout South Africa
exploded in a violent uprising, and black reporters, a number of
whom were by then working for the big white papers, began
risking their lives daily to get the story. All the black reporters on
the *Star* cited 1976 as a turning point in their lives. Whether they
were in school and politically involved or were already young
reporters, they were thrust into the crucible in 1976. With the
world's attention turning to Soweto and the other townships,
local black reporters were often the only source of news. The
government tried everything it could, including harassing, jailing, and torturing black journalists, to stifle press coverage of the
uprising. One day in 1976, Harry Mashabela, who had started at
the *Star* in 1964 as the first black reporter on a white paper, was
taken by the police directly from the *Star* newsroom to a Soweto
police station. As he was being led into an office, a senior police
officer suddenly punched him in the chest. At the same time,
another officer karate-chopped him from behind. The blow
dislocated his neck. Mashabela spent the next four months in a
police cell in excruciating pain, then was released without charges.
He had to have surgery for neck fusion, and the surgery saved his
life but left him with a permanently rigid neck and a very stiff
carriage. When he recounted this story to me in his office at the
Financial Mail, a weekly business magazine, where he was then
working, Mashabela, who is a soft-spoken, spindly, near-sighted

man, cheerfully named the policeman who almost killed him, and shrugged at the hopelessness of trying to sue for damages. He didn't shrug very well, though.

The families of detained journalists are often left in an agony of ignorance. Thami Mazwai, news editor of the *Sowetan*, was arrested in 1981. In 1983, his wife spoke to the Committee to Protect Journalists, whose report read, in part:

> Mrs. Mazwai had no idea where her husband was for the first few months he was detained. She went from one jail to another, hiding behind trees and shouting his name, until she traced him to Bloemfontein [in the Orange Free State, two hundred miles from Soweto]. Visiting two prisons a week, she found him after four months. Then, he was moved again. She found him in another jail in the eastern Transvaal, several hundred kilometers away from his Soweto home. By this time, he had been detained for seven months.

Thami Mazwai, who says that he was beaten while in jail, was finally released in late 1984.

Police harassment of black journalists normally seems to operate on an assumption that the reporters have useful information about the resistance and may be pleased to share it under prolonged interrogation; Joe Thloloe, of the *Sowetan*, was once held incommunicado for eighteen months. But it can also be simple, violent lashing-out. Montshiwa Moroke once went to cover a story about a group of squatters who were being evicted in Katlehong. The police attacked the squatters, then turned on the press. Moroke tried to escape in a car, but the police smashed all its windows. Moroke told me this story in a hushed voice one slow evening in the *Star* newsroom. He showed me a large scar on his head. "This is where they hit me with a sjambok. I didn't want to die in that car, so I got out. Then they really let me have it—they hit me everywhere. Finally, they dragged me over to their boss, who pointed his service revolver at me and said he was going to shoot. The cops were yelling, 'You are the cause of all this.' I didn't have the strength to ask them, 'How is the press the cause of squatting?' " The police commander did not shoot, but his men did throw Moroke, who was badly injured, into a police van that was already bursting with prisoners. Later, he lay in a police station for an hour before an ambulance was called. He was in the hospital for three weeks, off work for six weeks. An operation on a shattered elbow was a near-complete success. "Just sometimes, in the winter, it gets very sore, so that I can't write." Actually, Moroke carries the marks of police violence lightly. He is in his thirties, but he has a boyish quality—small and tidy, with the square shoulders and flat stomach of a teenager. He is watchful and quiet and widely read, and he seems to reveal his feelings about things only through his tireless reporting.

The police know how community pressures apply to black journalists. On the morning of the day I met Jon Qwelane, policemen had come to the *Star* newsroom looking for him. Luckily for him, he was not around. What they wanted, the policemen told his editor, was Qwelane's sources for a recent story about a shooting in the township of KwaThema. According to Qwelane's story, the shooting had occurred at a vigil for a woman who had died after being shot nine times by the police. Two men believed to be policemen fired six heavy-caliber bullets and several rounds of birdshot into the tent where the vigil was being held, killing a boy of fifteen and wounding one of sixteen. The police, Qwelane had reported, claimed to know nothing about the incident. "But they're not interested in who shot those kids," Qwelane told me. "They just want me to give them a name. Any name. Then they can go back to KwaThema and tell people I cooperated with them, and that will destroy my credibility. The whole idea is to embarrass you, and they win either way. If you don't name sources, you go to jail. If you name sources, you lose your credibility'.'

Being taken to court for refusal to name sources is such a common occupational hazard among black reporters that when I asked Mike Tissong about a suit the police were bringing against him—they wanted his sources for a story about seven youths in Duduza who were killed by booby-trapped hand grenades that a police plant posing as a guerrilla had given them—Tissong looked puzzled for a moment, and then his face fell. He had been so busy lately he had forgotten about the suit. It was an absurd case, Tissong said, because he had named his sole source in the story, and the police had already detained the poor guy. The police came back for Qwelane the next week, but they missed him again. "The boss told them to get lost," Qwelane said. "I just hope they do."

The Argus Company stands by its journalists when the state attacks them. Joe Thloloe has spent many years either banned or in detention; the company has paid him his salary throughout. Argus lawyers defend reporters whom the police have charged; they would be representing Mike Tissong in the Duduza case. When Phil Mtimkulu was banned for three years at the end of 1980, the company continued to pay his salary. This support flows, certainly, from the company's principles—Argus editors are among the country's leading defenders of the idea of a free press—but the importance of black journalists to news coverage in South Africa today is also hard to overstate. And the civil war raging in the townships has become, as Jon Qwelane says, "a world story."

"But look at how understaffed we are," Phil Mtimkulu said. "We get criticized for doing 'body count journalism,' and it's true. It's all we can do to cover the unrest as it's happening. We don't have the time to explore the background on stories. In many cases, too, we don't have the training."

Mtimkulu spent his years as a banned person working on a degree in African history through the University of South Africa, a correspondence college. (His banning was apparently related to his role as an officer in the Media Workers Association of South Africa, the black journalists' union, during a bitter two-month strike against the Argus Company.) He has since earned a second degree. Mtimkulu's nickname is "Doctor Malan"—sometimes just "Doc," or "Malan"—which he says he received from his parents, possibly because he was born in 1948, the year Dr. Malan led the National Party to power. It's a strange nickname indeed for a black South African, but it suits Mtimkulu somehow. He can be quite enigmatic, particularly if one does not speak Zulu. Very tall, very thin, very black and loose-limbed, Mtimkulu seems always to be in large, fluid motion, and, while I was around, he often seemed preoccupied with the avalanche of responsibilities that he faced as news editor of the Africa edition. And yet he retained a subtle, multilingual wit that regularly broke up his colleagues in the ghetto. On the rare occasions when he sat down in the newsroom to talk, he had the disconcerting habit of abruptly, without missing a beat in the conversation, dropping his adjustable chair to the floor. The effect was cartoonish—you expected him to speak suddenly in a different voice—and the more time I spent with Mtimkulu, the less I thought the effect was accidental.

Mtimkulu's defense of black reporters against the charge of doing "body count journalism" went on, typically, to challenge the reporters themselves. "The biggest problem is that most black reporters just don't have the confidence to break out and write other types of stories," he said. "We're quite good at going out and inhaling tear gas. But we've got to start showing we can do the more thoughtful writing, too. The op-ed pieces." Mtimkulu paused. Qwelane was knocking out a story on the next terminal. "Jon has really shown the way there," Mtimkulu said.

Chapter 7

Just Jon

Jon Qwelane is both a prolific reporter for the *Star*—his byline sometimes appears eight or ten times in a week, and on half a dozen different stories in the *Sunday Star*—and one of the paper's best-known columnists. He produces a steady stream of op-ed pieces, and when I was in Johannesburg he was writing two regular columns: "Jon's Jive," which appeared on Saturdays, and "Just Jon," on Sundays. Qwelane was then, in fact, the only black columnist writing for a white newspaper in South Africa.

Qwelane's weekly columns were in some ways his shelter from the storm of day-to-day reporting, and that was especially true of "Jon's Jive." "I try to keep that piece light," he told me. "There's too much gory stuff in the paper already. Sunday is the heavy one." For "Jon's Jive," he had written about everything from phantom loose pigs causing car accidents in Soweto to a variety of township slang known as *tsotsi taal*. He likes to set stories in shebeens, and often lets his Catholic schooling show in extravagant religious metaphors—even whole disquisitions on Heaven and Hell. These two leitmotifs, religion and drink, sometimes come together in a single column—like the one in which a drunkard, locked in shebeen debate with a priest, claimed that "some of the first drinks on record were mentioned in the Bible in the story of the wedding at Cana where guests were bored to tears because there was no hooch. The priest shot back that the biblical account nowhere stated that after the Lord converted water into wine, its drinkers got drunk."

The Saturday columns let Qwelane have fun with language. In another shebeen piece, a wife bursts in and starts belaboring her husband with a golf club. We listen to his pleading, her accusations, and in the midst of it are reminded, "All the time she was sinking putts with the club." The columns on township slang, of which there have been a number, celebrate the multilingual richness of their subject. A reader learns, for instance, that since money is "sugar," to be broke is to be "sugar-free"; that people of high standing are "situations," and their neighborhoods, should these also house poor residents, are "mink-and-manure townships"; that a "stop nonsense" is a concrete wall; that an irritating shebeen keeper may cause the customers to "impose economic sanctions." Some of these *tsotsi taal* columns read like an African *Finnegans Wake*, with the few conventional English words and phrases surfacing like small clear windows in a dense, jeweled cloud of language. In fact, they are much like urban African speech in South Africa, which one who does not understand the languages being used, but listens closely, finds studded with familiar bits: "unfortunately"s and "no matter what"s.

"Just Jon," Qwelane's Sunday column, may have been named that by the *Star*'s editors in the hope of reassuring white readers that the opinions expressed therein were the writer's own, not those of the newspaper—and not, heaven help us, those of blacks in general. As Rex Gibson says, "In some ways, Jon has come to be the symbol of all 'uppity kaffirs.' " Qwelane manages that trick simply by commenting on the issues of the day from a black perspective—not *the* black perspective, since there is no such thing, but a perspective that Gibson acknowledges "is very widespread," and that many whites seem to fear represents what their black workers or servants really think. In one of his first columns for the *Star*, Qwelane described how he and his friends were rooting against the white South Africans who were playing at

Wimbledon. The country's isolation in most international sports is a very sore point among white South Africans; the idea that "their" blacks might be enjoying their discomfiture is doubly enraging. After black spectators turned up at an international rugby match and cheered for the visiting squad, one Afrikaans newspaper angrily suggested that blacks wanting to attend future matches be screened to weed out subversives. Qwelane played straight to this weakness, and has continued ever since to insert the needle just where it hurts.

The angle of Qwelane's attacks on apartheid is different from that of the *Star*'s editorials: it emphasizes black experience rather than white guilt, and often projects a strange mock gaiety. Thus, when he slams P. W. Botha for betraying with the latest crackdown some vague promises of conciliation and "reform" that Botha made in a series of radio broadcasts and newspaper advertisements, he does so by way of an elaborate threat to sue the State President for false advertising.

At times, "Just Jon" is a straightforward editorial—one that may or may not follow the *Star*'s line. Qwelane, for instance, supports international economic sanctions against South Africa, and claims they have massive black support. Other columns are like megaphones: one side in the undeclared civil war speaking directly, angrily, to the other. When the white far right, spearheaded by the neo-Nazi Afrikaner Weerstandsbeweging (AWB), whose program includes a whites-only state, began to make their presence felt in white national politics, Qwelane wrote, "Perhaps the A.W.B. and its cronies are right about a white homeland, after all, and the sooner KwaWhitey is proclaimed, the better. All right-wingers must be told one thing: they are not as feared in the black community as they are in white circles."

The voluminous hate mail he receives, most of which he reads and keeps, lets Qwelane know his words are at least reaching the far side of the apartheid abyss. He once showed me a stack of letters—screeds full of death threats and psychopathic racism, most of them semiliterate, all of them unsigned—and said, with a short laugh, "Maybe I'll publish a selection someday. We could call it 'White Political Thinking.' " A few weeks before, Qwelane said, he had received a phone call from a woman, obviously white, who simply said, "You should be shot."

Though Qwelane is given fairly free rein by his editors in "Just Jon," he still has to battle to protect his copy. For instance, the *Star*, following government usage, calls the bantustans "home-lands," a term that Qwelane, like many blacks, rejects. So, to get "bantustan" past the copyeditors, he must put it inside a quote from a fictional conversation. (This may sound like a trivial problem, but terminology in South Africa is critical.) In any case, publishing Qwelane's columns is not a matter of altruism or political principle on the part of the *Star*. The newspaper not only heaps prestige upon itself by doing so, it also sells more papers. Qwelane's columns are hugely popular among blacks, and one white subeditor told me, "My mother absolutely hates Jon's writing, but she always reads his column first."

One of Qwelane's editors on the columns was Anita Hughes. A big, ebullient blonde young woman, she had worked with Qwelane for two years and was an outspoken admirer. "Jon's columns are so well thought out," she told me. "They always have a beginning, a middle, and an end. He writes to length, precisely. His copy is totally professional. His command of the English language, which isn't, after all, his native tongue, is superb. The only thing you might occasionally find is that he sometimes tends to be very adamant." As adamancy was also one of Anita Hughes's traits, she and Qwelane wrangled constantly. One of their standing differences was over his choice of work station. Hughes sat in the *Sunday Star* wing of the newsroom. One day while I was there, she strode into the ghetto and told Qwelane, obviously not for the first time, "We can't have you always sitting down here at this end. We want you up by us, where we can keep you nice and cool and calm." While Qwelane laughed and tried to change the subject, Montshiwa Moroke said to me, sotto voce, "She means where they can keep him *in check*." That day, Qwelane managed to divert Anita into an argument about whether Christ sjambokked the moneylenders in the temple— the Gospel according to Qwelane—or merely overturned their tables, as Hughes claimed. They went round and round, each wielding a considerable familiarity with the Bible, until Hughes finally exclaimed, "Every time I come down here, I stay two hours. Your mind is like a labyrinth. We have to sort you out!"

Rex Gibson was a Qwelane fan himself. "In his columns, you never get the feeling that he's writing to some hack formula, and he is consistently able to expose, with great effectiveness, the hypocrisy and shallowness of white arguments," Gibson told me. "Meanwhile, his straight reporting is of a very high caliber. He's a chameleon in that respect. He can leap from highly subjective comments to straight factual reporting." Of a recent story, broken by Qwelane after intensive investigation, on the violent activities of white vigilantes in West Rand townships, Gibson said, "We know he got it right, because if he'd got *anything* wrong we'd have heard all about it from the police." He paused, then added, "And somehow, through all this, Jon retains that great cheerfulness of his."

Several white *Star* reporters mentioned the same thing, in tones of grateful surprise, when I asked them about working with Qwelane: his warmth. Anita Hughes had been trying her hand at writing. She told me, "Every time I turned in a piece, Jon would write something encouraging about it and leave it in my 'desk' "—her personal computer file. Sheryl Raine, a labor reporter, described finding a computer-drawn house in her "desk" at Christmas, with a message from Qwelane, "Happy Christmas—Let's move into this house." "It was just such a lovely thing to do," she said.

Qwelane's connection to the *Star*'s computer system borders on the organic. Whenever we sat talking in the newsroom, he would chain-smoke cigarettes, drink can after can of Coca-Cola, answer the phone ("Newsroom," barked, might be followed by a quick conversation in South Sotho), and doodle on a computer terminal. Glowing patterns of dashes, commas, slashes, hyphens would slowly bloom across the screen, be abruptly cleared, then start growing up again. In the middle of a conversation, he would, to illustrate some point, turn to a monitor, call up a story, highlight a paragraph with a couple of key strokes, and say, "Read that." All activities in the vicinity of a terminal are marked by a steady flow of small inspirations—by Qwelane's casually making electronic notes to himself, reviewing the latest stories to come in, suddenly revising his own stories or columns, or leaving messages, both serious and playful, for his colleagues in their "desks." One white *Star* reporter said to me, "Jon is so locked into events and developments that it's as if the news has become fused with his personality. In fact, he's such a workaholic that if he ever stepped out of it suddenly he'd probably disintegrate."

This close relationship to his writing extends to Qwelane's reporting rounds, on which he is constantly canvassing public opinion—asking people what they think about the latest boycotts or killings or taxes. He conducts these open-ended surveys in taxis and buses and elevators and shops, addressing people in the African familiar mode as *buti* (brother), *mama* (mother), *sisi* (sister), or *baba* (father). The flow from these conversations into his columns can be startlingly direct. The passing comments of a cleaning woman may be recorded, turned into a witty attack on the government, and sent to his editor's "desk" in the space of an hour.

Archbishop Tutu is a Qwelane enthusiast—"I love Jon very much," he told me—but, unlike the reporter who believed that Qwelane would disintegrate if he took a break, Tutu thought he could use some time away from South Africa. "With the kind of reporting he does, he may need to have some of the poison drawn out of his system," Tutu said. "Maybe a stint overseas on a good paper."

There is, in fact, a whole array of overseas programs and fellowships, including the Nieman fellowship at Harvard, available to South African journalists, and these days they are more likely to be awarded to a black journalist than to a white. Qwelane is an obvious candidate for a Nieman, and he has been urged to apply for one, but he seems dubious. When I said I thought he could get one, he shrugged, and said, "I suppose I could join the jet set. But I just hate to be patronized."

At the moment, Qwelane is in no danger of joining the jet set. He lives in a tin-roofed four-room matchbox in a working-class district of Soweto called Chiawelo Extension Two, with his wife, Sana, and their two small children. The house has had electricity only since 1984; the toilet is an outhouse across the backyard. It is two taxi rides from the nearest supermarket, and almost twenty miles from Johannesburg. Sana, who is a quiet, powerful-looking woman with a lovely laugh, works as a nurse at a Johannesburg hospital. With their combined incomes, the Qwelanes have hopes of eventually building a bigger house—or building onto their present house. In the meantime, when Qwelane wants to write at home he must do so in longhand at the coffee table, which doubles as a dining-room table (and is, in fact, the only table in the house). It and two sofas, two chairs, a bookshelf, and a television set cram the tiny living room. "Desiderata" and an inexpensive print of Leonardo's "Last Supper" hang on the brick walls. On the bookshelf sit a Bible, a dictionary, a thesaurus, and several dozen Penguin paperbacks. Qwelane told me that the family doesn't keep any political literature in the house. (To do so is asking for trouble. Qwelane's good friend and colleague Montshiwa Moroke, who once collected books freely, lost his whole library in a police raid. Fortunately, he was not home when the police came, and when friends managed to reach him and warn him he simply abandoned the company car he was driving, and went into hiding. The other members of an activist theater group to which Moroke belonged were all arrested. He himself stayed underground for a year. It was when he finally, tentatively, resurfaced, half mad from running and hiding, that he first went to work as a journalist.)

Mudini Maivha and I went to the Qwelanes' for dinner one evening in June. It was a moonless night, but we hid my rented car behind the house anyway. There had been a lot of fighting in Chiawelo over the previous couple of weeks, with cars stolen, hijacked, and burned. It was not safe, moreover, to have a strange car parked in front of one's house—particularly not if anyone had seen a white man in that car. The Qwelanes' two-year-old son, Sobukwe—whom his father usually refers to as "this terrorist" or "this funnyman" or "this wild native" and, according to Sana, indulges hopelessly—was at his grandmother's house, in another district of Soweto, and their second child's birth was still some weeks away, so the house was quiet and peaceful.

Maivha, Qwelane, and I watched the news on television while Sana served dinner, which consisted of baked beans, a beef sausage called *boerewors,* and great helpings of mealie pap, the corn porridge that is the staple food of Africans throughout southern Africa. We washed the meal down with a sweet orange drink while P. W. Botha discoursed dourly on the screen about some rural water scheme. Then Deputy Minister of Information Louis Nel came on to warn us about ANC "terrorism."

"You know," Qwelane said, "no news story on South African television is complete without a Cabinet minister making some pronouncement on the subject. What kind of journalism is that?"

His point was immediately reinforced as Minister of Law and Order Louis Le Grange appeared, defending the latest extraordinary powers granted to the police, followed by the Home Affairs Minister, Stoffel Botha, announcing that he had just deported an American journalist (Richard Manning, of *Newsweek*). The next story was about locusts in the Orange Free State, and Maivha said, "I wonder what the Minister of Locusts will have to say." A few clips of World Cup soccer were shown, which Maivha and Qwelane watched intently. Soccer is easily the most popular sport among black South Africans, but SABC was not broadcasting the World Cup finals, which were being played that week. Instead, it was broadcasting rugby, a white sport, and tennis at Wimbledon, where the handful of "South African–born" or "South African–raised" players were being relentlessly featured.

When the news was over, Maivha, getting up to leave, asked Qwelane about his plans for the next day.

Qwelane said, "I think I will go around to some of the public toilets in town. I want to make sure they're still not letting niggers like you use the facilities. There could be a column in it."

Maivha, standing over Qwelane, who was sprawled on a couch, nodded slowly, suppressing a smile. "Good idea," he said. Then he thanked Sana, donned his lumberjacket, said "*Ciao*," and left on foot.

That evening, while we chatted, sipped coffee, ate ice cream, and watched TV, Qwelane was voluble and seemed relaxed—except that each time he heard a vehicle outside he fell silent. Now and then he went to the window, drew aside the heavy curtain, and looked out. A wild-looking boy had showed up at the *Star* that afternoon, appearing suddenly in the door of a conference room where Qwelane and I sat talking. The boy was a student leader, he was on the run, and he and some friends needed a place to stay that night. Qwelane had told him they couldn't stay at the house, but told me afterward that he expected them to turn up anyway. He just hoped they would come early; he didn't like opening the door after midnight, particularly not lately, when a strange car had been parked around the corner for several nights running, with men sitting in it.

I asked Qwelane if any of his neighbors had been firebombed. "Ye-e-e-es," he said. (Qwelane has a way of saying "yes" in a high, musical voice that makes it into at least a four-syllable word. The effect is to lighten the assertion, and to add some details without adding them. He also has a four-syllable "no" that is a whole conversation in itself.) "One of our neighbors just lost his home that way. Fortunately, no one was hurt or killed. But, you know, nothing is ever said. There is no warning. And after it happens you usually don't have to ask, 'Why did they hit me?' Because you already know. You paid your rent. You shopped in town. And the comrades have said they will enforce boycotts by petrol bombing."

Did he and Sana observe the boycotts?

"Of course. We have absolutely supported every consumer boycott, even when it meant going without the things that Sobukwe needed when he was very small. And we have stopped paying rent as well. Everyone in Soweto has."

Did his neighbors resent the comrades?

"People may fear the comrades, and they may dislike their methods—I don't agree with the tactics these kids use—but virtually every black person wants to see this country changed, wants to see the system overturned, and they know that is what the comrades are fighting for. The comrades are their children. People are proud of them. Everyone understands that they are up against a hell of a lot. You can't help admiring their courage."

The Qwelanes' neighborhood, which is made up of long rows of little houses exactly like theirs, is, in Qwelane's words, "a real old-time apartheid neighborhood," meaning that it dates from the days when areas of Soweto were, in effect, strictly segregated by language group—their neighborhood is still almost totally Venda-speaking. Qwelane moved there in 1983, after that policy had begun to unravel, and managed to get a ninety-nine-year lease on the house in 1984, when those became available. (Before that, virtually all Africans in urban areas were forced to rent housing—if they could find it—from the government.) "Most of our neighbors are conservative, rural people," Qwelane told me. "The women wear traditional Venda headdresses, which can be quite elaborate, and all kinds of leg bracelets. In fact, their legs look like very well-fed pythons. On Sunday afternoons, the neighbors all get together in the field just here next to us and have a party. They beat drums, blow whistles, play guitars, dance. And the hooch flows! It all gets so loud you can't believe it. I call it the Venda National Symphony Orchestra. As soon as it starts, I flee. I go to see friends."

Qwelane's friends, who tend to be other journalists, mostly live in other sections of Soweto, some of them many miles away. When they get together, they speak English. "But I often wonder why," Qwelane once said to me. "What's wrong with our own languages? We are not Englishmen." The language spoken around the Qwelanes' house is Zulu, Sana's mother tongue. So Zulu will be Sobukwe's mother tongue, too. He is also picking up some Venda from the little girl next door. And some Sotho from the neighbor kid at his grandmother's house. And English from his parents and their friends. When he reaches school age, Jon and Sana plan to send him to St. Joseph's College, a Catholic boarding school in Botswana, which Jon himself attended.

Jon was born and raised in Mafeking, a small railway-junction town in the northern Cape. Perhaps because his childhood co-incided with the somber heyday of grand apartheid—that period when the government first moved to impose its gigantic, mon-strous plan of racializing and revamping every aspect of South African society—the outlines of his early life as he recalls it seem etched largely by political developments. The apartheid program of "forced removals," which has displaced three and a half mil-lion people to date, included the destruction of the "native loca-tion" outside Mafeking where the Qwelanes lived. Jon remembers the destruction of his family's home, and the scatter-ing of his extended family. The introduction of the system known as Bantu Education, under which the government took over responsibility for black education from the churches and openly proclaimed that its intention was to provide blacks with perma-nently inferior schooling, also affected Qwelane directly and lastingly. His father was a teacher, and a graduate of All Saints College, which had been one of the top black schools under the old mission system. Proud, strict, politically aware, the elder Qwelane was so appalled by Bantu Education that he quit his job, left South Africa to teach in neighboring Botswana (then still the British protectorate of Bechuanaland), and sent seven of his nine children to school there.

The education that Qwelane received at St. Joseph's, which he attended on a half-scholarship, was academically superior in ev-ery way to what was being offered to his peers at home in South Africa, but was probably most valuable simply for its retention of English as the medium of instruction. Under Bantu Education, a program of "mother-tongue instruction" had been imposed on African schools, requiring the use of African vernacular lan-guages in all subjects for the first eight years of schooling. Mother-tongue instruction is one of the pillars of the apartheid program of "retribalization," and its effect on black education has been devastating. Not only are the African languages unsuitable for learning basic subjects such as science, mathematics, history, and geography, but the few children who reach high school are desperately unprepared to suddenly start learning in English or Afrikaans. The majority who never reach high school are, of course, unprepared for life in modern society, except in the most menial capacities. Qwelane escaped the debilitation of Bantu Education. What is more, the colonial and parochial education he received, for all its shortcomings, allowed his aptitude for English to flower.

Qwelane spent his school holidays in Mafeking, however, and most of his childhood memories are distinctly South African. He and his friends would carry bundles of laundry for the washerwomen of the "location" into the white town, and Qwelane remembers being set upon there by gangs of white boys and beaten up, for reasons he could never fathom. His mother was an uneducated, devout Catholic who worked as a domestic servant and took no interest in politics; he remembers her simple pride in the fact that she worked for the family of the chief magistrate of Mafeking. ("If you have read P. G. Wodehouse," he has written, "you will know that such seemingly inconsequential social distinctions mean a lot in the servants' quarters.")

His father, meanwhile, conveyed his own political convictions to his children. He refused to call white men, even policemen who demanded his pass, *baas*—he once went to jail for objecting to the way the police addressed him—and when shop assistants treated him badly he took his business elsewhere. He also taught his children a version of South African history not found in the official texts: "My father always made it clear that this was the black man's land, that it was stolen from him." His political hero was Robert Mangaliso Sobukwe, a brilliant African nationalist who had also once been a schoolteacher. Sobukwe, founder of the Pan-Africanist Congress, is one of the tragic figures in South African history. He was jailed for incitement for three years in 1960, and held for six more years without charges (the longest anyone has ever been imprisoned without charges in South Africa), then confined to his home in Kimberley under a banning order, until he died, from cancer, in 1978. Jon Qwelane's father died in 1967. Qwelane's naming his own firstborn Sobukwe honored both Robert Mangaliso Sobukwe and his father.

"I got into journalism by accident, really," Qwelane told me. "After high school, I was working as a clerk at the Department of

Health and Social Welfare in Mafeking. There was a weekly
paper, the Mafeking *Mail*, with a black edition that consisted of
a four-page supplement that was mostly sports. A relative of the
editor told me they needed a freelance sportswriter, so I started
filling in for them. I did that for four or five months—this was
1972. Then I started sending in freelance articles about local
politics to the *Rand Daily Mail*. They bought everything I sent
them, so I took heart and, in 1974, moved to Jo'burg. I had no
prospects when I arrived, but fortunately I had quite a number
of aunts and uncles in the area. I stayed with an uncle in Soweto,
and after a short while I got a job with the *World*"—a black
paper—"covering news and courts. But I was too wild to stay
with that uncle and his family. He was a very conventional man,
and I kept no schedule—I slept at the office, I slept in shebeens—
so we fell out after just three months. Really, I was an untamed
rogue at that time."

Freelance sportswriting was the traditional portal into black
journalism, and Qwelane's performance as a young reporter in
Johannesburg was also in the high tradition of *Drum* and the
Golden City Post. The untamed rogue from Mafeking moved,
wrote, and drank at a ferocious pace, careering from paper to
paper in what sounds today like one long hurricane of scoops and
sprees. From the *World* (which was banned in 1977, resurrected
as the *Post*, banned again in 1980, then resurrected again as the
Sowetan) he went to the *Sunday Times*, a paper with a huge
circulation and an especially insulting extra edition, for which
Qwelane covered news and sports. He found he liked the deadlines on a weekly (they gave him more time to carouse), and set
the pattern for his next several jobs by celebrating a streak of
exemplary reporting and page-one bylines with a binge that
ended in a smashed company car and abrupt unemployment.

In 1976, the Afrikaans papers were desperate for coverage of
the uprising taking place in the townships, and so Qwelane went
to work for *Beeld,* the Johannesburg morning daily. He was the
first—"and still, as far as I know, the only"—black reporter to
work there. "That was a hair-raising experience," he told me.
"But I discovered that some of those chaps, despite being Afri-

kaners, have a lot of integrity. I wrote in English, they translated my copy, *and they never changed the meaning at all*. They actually wanted to know what was happening. I had front-page stories so many days. The funny part was that the people in the townships didn't mind that I was working for *Beeld*. Things were much less polarized then. The people were not so critical of the press."

After several months of hard and dangerous reporting and then a week's unauthorized vacation in a *Beeld* car, Qwelane found himself back on the sidewalk. He next went to work for the *Citizen*—"This was before anything was known about that paper's funding"—where he was again the only black reporter. The stint was a short one, ending the same way as the others. The *Rand Daily Mail* hired Qwelane in 1977. There he escaped the sports beat once and for all when an editor assigned him to cover a boxing match after he had gone to a friend's wedding. Soweto weddings often involve some drinking. By the time Qwelane got to the fight, which was a title bout, he "couldn't tell a left hook from a push." His report reflected this confusion, and news became his only beat thereafter. The two years he spent on the country's leading English-language newspaper sharpened Qwelane's skills as a journalist, but they did not mend his ways. His tenure at the *Mail* ended after a misunderstanding with the security guards at the paper's offices. "They handcuffed me and beat me up quite well," he said. "Afterward, it was their word against mine about what happened, and there were six of them and no witnesses."

Then there came a one-day stint at *Drum*. The magazine was only a shadow of its former electrifying self, but Jim Bailey, its longtime owner, still prized racy writing, for which Qwelane had become known. On the afternoon of the day he was hired, the staff held "a welcoming piss-up." Qwelane's memory of the party is sparse, but the editors afterward helped him piece together a version of events that featured him accusing Jim Bailey of giving him drinks in order to kill him, the same way he had killed Casey Motsisi, Can Themba, and other bright lights of the Golden Era.

The suggestion hurt Bailey deeply, and he fired Qwelane on the spot. Qwelane apologized, but was not rehired.

Qwelane joined the *Star* in 1979. His drinking, superb reporting, and insubordination continued until one day in 1982. "I went to cover a story and came back the story itself—the story of the newsroom," he said. "Smashed to hell and beyond." He was fired, and then, after three months, rehired on condition that he reform. Qwelane stopped drinking, relapsed, and stopped again, off and on for a year or so. Finally, in 1983, he joined a Soweto chapter of Alcoholics Anonymous. The group meets every Sunday. He never misses a meeting. Qwelane runs down the rap sheet of his decade as the bad boy of Johannesburg newsrooms with a sort of rueful relish. At the same time, there is something automatic about his confession: the slight dissociation of the consciously cured.

In his nine years at the *Star*, Qwelane has covered many beats and a great range of stories: township politics, bantustan politics, mine disasters, hospital scandals, hailstorms and car accidents, political trials, and the Soweto Scrabble craze. He has interviewed or profiled most of the leading figures in black politics: Nelson Mandela, Winnie Mandela, Desmond Tutu, Chief Gatsha Buthelezi. From the beginning, Qwelane showed a flair for feature writing. He could write features that were strictly "human interest": on the Jews of Soweto; on young black artists; a panoramic, Dickensian description of the black wing of the Johannesburg train station at Christmas, with vivid descriptions of pickpockets and of young migrant workers going home with their new clothes and radios. He could write features with political themes: visits to the families of political prisoners, an analysis of black student organizations, the meaning of funerals in black society.

Qwelane became known for his inventive, cinematic leads. In a story about a boxing champion sentenced to death for murder, Qwelane's opening focused on the guppies in the fish tank beside the TV set in the boxer's mother's flat—how even they seemed to swim dejectedly. In his straight political reporting, the tension between his subjects and his own political views often gave his stories a special tautness; and the underpinnings of that tension were sometimes revealed in the separate editing his pieces received for the white and the black editions of the *Star*. Thus, Qwelane's account of a Buthelezi speech in Soweto (Buthelezi, the leader of KwaZulu, the large and heavily populated bantustan for Zulu speakers, is in favor among the *Star*'s editors) emphasized in the white editions the Zulu strongman's anti-government remarks, while in the Africa edition it emphasized Buthelezi's belligerence toward black journalists and his penchant for making silly remarks. (Figures less popular with the *Star*'s editors could be treated less delicately: a Qwelane profile of Ephraim Tshabalala, "mayor" of Soweto and a supporter of the government, took little trouble to mask its writer's scorn for its subject.) In 1983, Qwelane got his first column. It was called "My Word" and ran only in the *Star*'s Africa edition. The column gave him new freedom not only as a writer but as a political commentator. When he wrote about bantustan leaders in his column, Qwelane simply eviscerated them.

With a regular column in the *Star*, Qwelane's work became widely known—particularly after his column started to run in the paper's white editions—but he continued to work as a field reporter, and is perhaps still best-known for a remarkable series of stories he filed in March and April of 1985. On March 21, the police opened fire on a crowd marching near Uitenhage, in the eastern Cape; twenty-one people were killed and hundreds wounded. Qwelane flew to the eastern Cape that day, and the next day he filed a story that challenged police claims about the killing. Louis Le Grange, the Minister of Law and Order, had told Parliament that petrol bombs were being used against police before the shooting. Qwelane searched the length of the road where the shooting took place, and "found neither splinters of glass nor anything to indicate that petrol had burned on the surface." He gathered eyewitness accounts disputing official assertions that freedom songs were being sung, political slogans chanted, and a warning to disperse given before the police opened fire. (A government investigation later found that the police had lied.) The next day, he reported allegations by the Uitenhage Black Civic Organization that police had shot and killed people who were lying wounded on the ground, and had then placed stones beside their bodies to suggest that they had been throwing them.

"It was supposed to be an in-and-out thing," Qwelane told me. "But I saw that there was a hell of a story still developing, so I stayed. I ended up staying four weeks." The residents of Langa, the township where the shooting had occurred, and of the nearby township of KwaNobuhle were in an insurrectionary mood after the massacre. Both townships were sealed off by police road-blocks, memorial services were banned, all black policemen and their families were evacuated, and residents staged mass stay-aways from work. Mobs controlled the streets, especially at night, and Qwelane was soon the only journalist left on the scene. He had to work incognito, moving around on foot, taking no notes, doing his utmost to avoid being noticed either by police or by angry crowds. He was filing his stories over the phone, straight out of his head, and, unbeknownst to him, they were being run by the entire Argus group and picked up by newspapers around the world. Each phone he used went dead shortly after he used it and brought police swarming, but Qwelane kept moving, using different phones. When Bernardus Fourie, the South African ambassador to the United States, said on American television that cannibalism was taking place in the Uitenhage townships, Qwelane was in position to file a story citing numerous sources and headlined "CANNIBALISM REPORTS DENIED."

Qwelane saw his share of horrors, however. At the end of his first week in Langa, he estimated that ten people had been "burned to death by angry crowds in the last four days." His eyewitness account of the death of one township councillor, T. B. Kinikini, probably made such events more real than many of his readers were prepared for. But the most extraordinary story that Qwelane filed from Langa was the one headlined, in the Star's Africa edition, "RELUCTANT HEADHUNTER'S NIGHT

OF TERROR." It described his being press-ganged into a mob that was going from house to house demanding that all able-bodied males join the search for a businessman it had decided to burn. The tone of the story was half farce, half nightmare as it told of Qwelane's marching around with the mob, praying that it would find no one to kill. That night, his prayers were answered: "Just as I began thinking there was no way out, reason prevailed. Our unseen commander suddenly considered the possibility of an encounter with the law, and wondered what the outcome would be. A murmur of voices, including mine, forecast dire consequences and after more talking we were ordered to disband, each on honorable discharge."

The next evening, Qwelane had an even more frightening experience. The mob came again to the house where he was staying, again looking for the businessman, but this time someone suddenly decided that the stranger, Qwelane, was the man it sought. "There were about two hundred men out there, with knives, spades, axes, and a jerrycan full of petrol," Qwelane recalled. "Some of them were shouting, 'Your time is up!' and 'You bastard!' and 'You've sold us out long enough!' They were holding on to me, and they were shining a big torch in my eyes, so that I couldn't see. I tried to stay calm and collected. It was no time to start feeling sorry for myself. I showed them my air ticket back to Johannesburg, and my press card—which almost made matters worse, because it mentions the Commissioner of Police on it, and somebody noticed that. What saved me was the people I was staying with. One is an ex-detainee, the other is a former Robben Island prisoner. The crowd decided that such people would not have a sellout in their house. But a mob is almost impossible to reason with, you know. It only takes one irresponsible accusation these days to seal your doom."

Qwelane nevertheless stayed on in Langa, chronicling the disintegration of state authority in the Uitenhage townships, the spreading of violent resistance to nearby "coloured" areas, and the squabbling that broke out between local political organizations and trade unions in the heat of the confrontation. His descriptions of the horrible living conditions in the Uitenhage townships gave added context to the uprising; his report on the mass funeral in KwaNobuhle, where more than seventy thousand mourners turned out to bury twenty-nine dead, conveyed the scale and the focus of events; and his ongoing investigation of the massacre on March 21 continued to undermine police statements.

But it was the close call with the mob in Langa that seemed to remain with most of his colleagues—who often told me to "ask Jon about Uitenhage" or to look up the stories he had filed from there—as the scene that summed up the assignment. For it also summed up their own dilemma: how to mediate between their duties as newsmen, their powerful identification with the struggle for black liberation, and their understandable alarm, both personal and political, over the forms that struggle can take.

After Qwelane's harrowing stint in Uitenhage, the *Star*'s editors rewarded him with a trip to Europe. As he recalls it, the trip was less than a life's dream come true. "They managed to get me a passport, so I thought I should go. Very few of the chaps can get passports, and it was a chance to get the word out." He went to London, Amsterdam, and Paris, filing travel pieces and columns (including one claiming that he could not relax in places where there were white street sweepers and white hotel porters, and white policemen who called him "sir," and concluding, "No, something is seriously wrong with overseas people"), and doing some public speaking, but mostly visiting exiles, many of them journalists or ex-journalists who were old friends.

Exile has been the fate of a dizzying number of black South African journalists. They live all over Africa, Europe, and America, teaching, writing, working in the outlawed liberation movements. Many fail to cope: Nat Nakasa threw himself out a window in New York; Can Themba drank himself to death in Swaziland. "Even the ones who are doing well seemed so homesick, so out of place," Qwelane told me. "The chap I stayed with in Paris got out and played some old jazz records that he used to love as a kid in Alexandra, and you never saw such pain in a man's face. He's working in radio now. His kids speak French; they go to a French school."

Later that year, Qwelane visited the United States. "In Newark, New Jersey, we had a party the night before I was supposed to fly back," he told me. "There must have been fifteen exiles there, including Joe Gumede, who's my journalistic grandfather. You see, he brought Joe Thloloe into journalism, who, years later, brought me in. Joe Gumede works at the United Nations now. That was a great party—it went all night and I ended up missing my flight—but it was also so sad. Some of the guys were literally crying at the thought of mothers whom they had not seen in twenty-five years. They were all giving me messages to take home. They *missed* the ghetto. No, man, exile looks too sad."

Occasionally, Qwelane talks about the possibility of being forced to leave South Africa himself. On that June evening in his living room in Chiawelo Extension Two, he sighed, and said, "I think I'll only skip if I'm facing five years or more. That long in jail is just such a waste of time."

The student leader and his comrades didn't show up at Qwelane's that night. We watched *The Golden Girls*, a program that Qwelane loves—the only one he watches regularly besides *The Cosby Show*. He chuckled at every laugh line as the aging southern belle played by Rue McClanahan tried to decide whether to marry the dashing millionaire who had flown her to Atlanta in his private jet for dinner. Later, in the middle of a serious conversation about socialism and the Book of Exodus, with Sana still watching TV, Qwelane noticed something on the screen and interrupted himself. "It's Hagar!" he cried. "I love Hagar." We turned and watched. It was a commercial, a cartoon, with a Viking curmudgeon selling flashlight batteries.

It was nearly midnight when I finally rose to head back to town. An old black-and-white Tarzan movie was just starting. There was tribal dancing—Africans imitating birds in a furious mating dance—intercut with some glittering repartee among the khaki-clad white folk looking on. Jon and Sana saw me to my car before Tarzan appeared. They told me—almost pleaded with me—to stop for nothing and no one until I was out of Soweto. I managed to follow their advice as far as the Army roadblock at the edge of the township, where I had no choice but to stop. The young white soldiers peered at me for a long moment, cradling their automatic rifles. They seemed frightened as they waved me on.

Chapter 8

The Whiteness
of the <u>Star</u>

Since Jon Qwelane is so widely liked at the *Star*, and his abilities are so widely acknowledged (an American reporter working temporarily at the *Star* on an exchange program told me, "Jon's advice on how to do a story here has been worth more to me than what all the editors put together could offer"), a question naturally arises about his status at the paper. It arises especially often among his black colleagues. Maud Motanyane told me, "They've misused Jon a hell of a lot. His columns contribute enormously to the paper, but he's not getting the credit. There're so few white reporters at the *Star* even close to Jon in experience or ability." A white colleague put the situation more bluntly: "If he were white, Jon Qwelane would be much higher at the paper. As it is, there's really nowhere for him to go."

During the time I spent at the *Star*, Phil Mtimkulu was, as far as I could tell, the only black editor on a white newspaper in South Africa, and his job—news editor of the Africa edition—was near the bottom of the *Star*'s large editorial pile. All the subeditors were white. All the assistant editors were white. All the editors were white.

When I asked Rex Gibson about the situation, he said, "It's in a way an indictment of the newspaper, but it's much more an indictment of this country's educational system. We don't want tokenism. It's one of our great dilemmas." Gibson is a short, white-bearded, well-spoken man with sharp eyes and a merry face. His large, wood-paneled office overlooked a downtown street into which poured and dispersed, four times a day, fleets of trucks, vans, and bicycles, all emblazoned with the *Star*'s motto, "The Star TELLS IT LIKE IT IS," and bearing full loads of the latest edition. When we spoke, Gibson mentioned Qwelane and Mtimkulu as having "the potential" to rise to higher positions at the paper, insisted that equal opportunity was already a reality at the *Star*, and pointed out that race barriers have been broken down more quickly at newspapers than elsewhere in South Africa.

Anita Hughes seconded her editor's view that there was no racial discrimination in promotion at the *Star*, but also suggested the role of apartheid—of white-minority rule—in the editorial department's structure when she expanded on her point. "Jon sometimes jokes about what he'll do when he's the editor, and who knows, it could happen. There could be a black editor here someday, giving orders to the white staff. Who knows what might happen after the revolution!" Hughes's tone made it clear that she did not expect (or desire) to see such a change soon.

Rex Gibson's point about the educational disadvantages suffered by black journalists is well taken. White journalists in South Africa, including the editors of major newspapers, tend not to have gone to college themselves. In South Africa, as on Fleet Street, journalists, at least traditionally (this is becoming less true), start at the bottom as teenagers and move up on moxie and skill. But even the basic ration of formal education that all of them received exceeds significantly what their black colleagues have. (Qwelane's schooling in Botswana largely, but not entirely, exempts him from this problem.) The fact that English is a second or third language for most black journalists is another major disadvantage. An inadequate English vocabulary causes some black reporters to rely on extravagant language that can then be read by editors as deliberate exaggeration. Yet, even when they employ the most restrained language, black reporters on white newspapers seem to stand permanently suspected by their editors of exaggeration, especially in their unrest coverage—of an inability to be "objective."

Allister Sparks, former editor of the *Rand Daily Mail*, says the suspicion is justified. "It's an absurd expectation, that they be objective. It would be like sending a Jew out to cover politics in Germany in the 1930s and expecting him to be completely detached about all this Nazi business." Sparks, who was often accused of tokenism for his attempts to promote blacks at the *Mail*, has come to see inherent problems in such promotions. "The upper ranks on a newspaper require a cool, analytic approach, while the emotional pressures in the townships make that almost impossible to develop. You, your family, your neighbors, your friends, are being harassed, imprisoned, killed. . . . If we are going to overcome this problem, we must identify the right individuals early and bring them along, being very careful not to get anyone labeled as the white man's boy, because when he starts giving orders, when he acts analytical—telling reporters, 'Take out these adjectives,' that sort of thing—he may seem like a sellout." (Sparks and I had this conversation at his home outside Johannesburg, overlooking the swimming pool, tennis court, and grounds to whose loveliness no adjectives can possibly do justice. I hadn't felt so analytical in weeks. But the Telex in Sparks's study suddenly started rattling about a wave of raids, arrests, and disappearances, and our interview was cut short.)

Ultimately, the reason blacks do not occupy positions of editorial power at a newspaper like the *Star* is that, politically and economically, it is a white paper, and the interests of blacks and whites in South Africa are, in many ways, at this point in history, simply fundamentally different. Black readership is large—that is why the Africa edition exists—but whites, who control most of the disposable income in the country, are the main targets of the *Star*'s advertisers. They are the paper's financial raison d'être. Naturally, they, in combination with the paper's ownership, determine the *Star*'s outlook. No newspaper can survive that does not reflect in large measure the views of its readers.

Who are the owners of the *Star*? Basically, they are the same people who own South Africa's mineral wealth. These well-fixed individuals are usually described by foreign analysts as "English financial interests," by local Marxists as "big capital," and by a broad spectrum of South Africans simply as "Anglo"—short for the Anglo American Corporation, a consortium that dominates the national economy, controlling directly or indirectly a breathtaking number of companies (over half the companies on the Johannesburg Stock Exchange, in fact), the Argus Company among them.

It is an oversimplification to say that the English-language press and the liberal opposition party in the whites-only Parliament, the Progressive Federal Party, are Anglo mouthpieces, end of story, but the links between the three groups and the convergence of their interests are certainly thoroughgoing. Anglo has long financed the Progressive Federal Party; the government press regularly refers to the *Star* and its sister papers as "the PFP press"; and the political positions of party and press are essentially the same: anti-apartheid, but opposed to one-person, one-vote in a unitary state (the political structure favored by an overwhelming majority of blacks), or to any other form of majority rule that does not safeguard "minority rights" (a phrase that means different things to different people, but is widely suspected among blacks to be a euphemism for white privilege). The *Star* provides abundant news space and op-ed space to PFP spokesmen, Anglo's top managers, and other leading businessmen, and editorially never questions the sincerity of their views— although cynicism about the anti-apartheid protestations of groups like Anglo American, whose profits have always depended on the crude neo-slavery of the migrant labor system (a far more fundamental feature of apartheid than, say, laws concerning sex or marriage across the color line), runs extremely deep throughout South Africa.

Actually, "free enterprise," rather than "minority rights," has been the main theme of the white opposition's political pronouncements recently, and one gets the impression that Anglo's managers don't necessarily fear a black government in South

Africa; they make healthy profits, after all, from their many mines in independent Africa. What they fear is a socialist government—particularly one that might nationalize their holdings. This concern was undoubtedly on the agenda of the historic discussions held, much to the displeasure of the Botha government, between representatives of Anglo American and the ANC at ANC headquarters in Lusaka, Zambia, in 1986. Earlier in this century, the English-language press proudly declared itself to be the political voice of the great mining houses. That this relationship is no longer proclaimed in print may have at least something to do with a long-term divergence of interests between the mineowners and the *Star*'s white readers, who as a group decidedly still fear the idea of a black government. In any case, the *Star*'s political position must mediate between these groups— groups whose politics have little in common with the politics of the black resistance, to which all black journalists broadly subscribe.

Basic issues, basic institutions—Parliament, the South African military, the country's international relations—are seen from virtually opposite angles by the *Star*'s white editors and its black reporters. Thus, the paper's foreign correspondents file (and the editors publish) bitter, panicky stories about "anti-S.A. demos" in Britain and America, while black South Africans on the whole, and certainly all the black journalists I've ever met, see the same protests as being anti-*apartheid*, in *support* of the majority of South Africans, and welcome the news of them.

The *Star*'s "political correspondent," stationed in Cape Town to cover Parliament, has the sort of high-profile, senior reporting job that Jon Qwelane might seem to be in line for—except that the political correspondent couldn't possibly be black. Not only would covering the Nationalist-dominated Parliament be difficult, if not impossible, because of some of the petty-apartheid laws and the racism of most M.P.s, but the correspondent's analyses of events, whether labeled as such or implied in his reporting, must at least take the parliamentary issues and debates seriously, and also reflect the *Star*'s political line—things that no black reporter could credibly do.

Military correspondent is also out. One Saturday while I was in Johannesburg, the South African armed forces paraded their troops and weaponry through the city's streets. The *Sunday Star* sent half a dozen photographers and reporters to the parade, including Qwelane. A full page of color photographs and a story describing the parade in stupefying detail appeared in the next day's paper. Qwelane, one of the few blacks in the crowd that lined the route, declined to contribute to the staff-written story, but produced his own report, focusing on a conversation overheard between two young blacks, the essence of which was that this parade was nothing compared to the daily military displays to be seen in Soweto. Qwelane's story was spiked. White South Africans, on the whole, passionately support the South African military. It represents them, it defends them. Black South Africans, on the whole, just as passionately hate the South African military. It is the enemy's army. This fundamental opposition is clearly acknowledged in the law that makes military service compulsory for white males and only white males. The *Star*, as a white newspaper, might question some of the military's activities, but it would never question its legitimacy. To do so would be unpatriotic. (The white South African concept of "patriotism" is itself meaningless to most black South Africans.) When the South African Air Force unveiled its new Cheetah fighter jet in 1986 (and *Beeld*'s headline howled, "NOW LET THE MIGS COME!"), a PFP politician who did not wish to be named said in the *Star*, "It's hard not to feel pride in what the South African armaments industry is producing." This difficulty was clearly exclusive to whites.

The list of subjects that the *Star*'s white editors and black reporters approach from opposite sides goes on, and ends up casting the question of black promotion in a purely political light. When I asked Phil Mtimkulu about his prospects for promotion to assistant editor, he shook his head. "You would have to react to things so unnaturally," he said, "If bombs go off, an assistant editor must say, 'Violence won't help!' If it's sanctions, he must say, 'Sanctions won't help!' But if you believe violence *will* help, sanctions *will* help . . ." Assistant editors (along with the editor

himself) write the *Star*'s editorials. Black reporters, even respected senior journalists like Mtimkulu and Qwelane, are never
consulted about their content. Maud Montanyane said, "You
might think they would at least want to ask us about things they
know nothing about, but have to write about, such as black
housing. They never do, though."

Qwelane claims not to be interested in a promotion; indeed, he
seemed to shudder at the suggestion. "No," he said. "I'm just one
of the boys here. I have no ambition to become an editor. In fact,
I hate authority, I hate discipline, so I can't see anybody else not
hating me in that capacity. I see myself as a storyteller." He
turned and started tapping slowly, thoughtfully, at a keyboard:
the African storyteller at his computer terminal. Phil Mtimkulu
said of Qwelane, "He is not an executive type of guy. He's a
writer." But it was on Mtimkulu's behalf, and on Maud Motanyane's, that Qwelane could get vehement about the lack of equal
opportunity for blacks at the *Star*. He thought their talent was
unappreciated at the paper, "and it's just color, nothing more."
Of himself, he said, "The *Star*'s been good to me. Come to think
of it, I can't think of anyone, black or white, who has been given
more chances than me." At the time I was in Johannesburg,
Qwelane was earning sixteen hundred rands (about seven hundred dollars) a month, but he said, somewhat sheepishly, "Even
if I were being paid two hundred rands, I suppose I would still
be doing this job. I suppose it's just love of the game."

In the years he has worked there, Qwelane has seen the *Star*
change considerably. When he started, the paper's black reporters were still compelled to eat in a segregated canteen, "using
zinc plates and zinc mugs, like the sort of thing you find in jail."
(When Harry Mashabela started, fifteen years earlier, he was
forced to cover stories from a messenger's motorbike, because in
those days the *Star*'s drivers were white and the transport manager would not have white men driving a black man around.)
The paper's editorial line was much more conservative. For that
matter, the editorial stance of every large white newspaper in
South Africa is far less openly racist than in the past, and that of
the English press less colonial—no longer do the English papers

refer to "natives," or call England "home," as the *Star* still did not so long ago. The recent calls by Argus papers for the legalization of the ANC, and a new willingness to quote ANC leaders, reflect a growing realism on the part of the liberal press about the state of South African politics. Qwelane applauds this shift at the *Star*. "The paper used to be a fence sitter," he told me. "But the pressures on it were increased by the closing of the *Rand Daily Mail*, which has helped to put the *Star*'s responsibilities to the public more and more in focus. Right now, the paper is a very audible voice for change." At the same time, Qwelane is openly critical of the politics of the *Star*'s editors. "They always keep an eye over their right shoulder, just like the government does. The government watches the white right wing. They watch their advertisers. And when you come down to it, those guys in the mahogany room don't want a majority government in this country. They just want a more humane white order."

The situation of white liberals in South Africa recalls the Helen Hokinson cartoon in which a sweet-faced, ample-bosomed Connecticut clubwoman in a sun hat, addressing a group of similar women, says, "Of course, we must draw some sort of distinction between wishing to overthrow the government and not liking the present administration." Reporters on the English papers actually talk sometimes about the ur-reader whom their editors want them to address as "the lady on the Kensington bus." A *Star* editorial in March, 1986, caught the paper's vaguely Victorian disquiet perfectly when, after hailing the government's most recent reform initiatives, it declared, "The hope must be that, meanwhile, all other volatile socio-political elements at work in the country can be reasonably contained." (A daily column called "Stoep Talk"—porch talk—expresses this lace-curtain sensibility in perhaps its purest form. In May, 1986, the civil war raging in Alexandra found its way into "Stoep Talk" in the form of a story headed "ALEX HIJACKING LEAVES ANIMAL BODY IN DISTRESS." The story read, in part: "The Society for Animals in Distress suffered a devastating blow in Alexandra Township this week when a group of young boys hijacked one of its vans, drove it away and left it a burnt-out wreck. . . . A heartbroken Mrs.

Didi Rutherford, vice chairman of the society, said the total loss
in financial terms was enormous . . . . The animals in Alex were
suffering because the society's vans had not been able to go in on
a regular basis.")

Bishop Tutu, when we spoke, said, "I gave the *Rand Daily
Mail* seven out of ten. I give the *Star* three out of ten. Like most
white people, they want change just as long as things remain the
same." (Tutu had a personal beef with the white opposition
press. As he told me, "I'm the ogre at the moment for whites,
which means that Tutu-bashing helps these papers curry favor
with whites. So they do it endlessly." Tutu was even talking
about suing the *Star* over an article that called him "a theological
impostor.") Ameen Akhalwaya, the editor of *The Indicator*, the
innovative opposition knock-and-drop, dismissed the *Star* as
"just a white man's paper, with a huge colonial hangover." Even
Joe Thloloe, an utterly genial man despite his many years of
prison and banning, seemed to deliberately overlook the modernization of racial terminology when we spoke in his office at the
Sowetan. He said, "The attitude of the English press is, 'We
shouldn't be so cruel to our natives. We can get the same results
much more humanely.' "

The major organizations of black resistance, the United Democratic Front and the Azanian Peoples' Organization (AZAPO),
generally regard the white liberal press in the same light as they
do the South African Parliament—as legitimizing, through its
tolerated opposition to the government, a fundamentally illegit-
imate system; as, in the words of one AZAPO official, "the ruling
class giving itself a veneer of democracy" while propagating "the
values of international imperialism and capitalism." The hostility
of even liberal editors to organizations like AZAPO and the
UDF, let alone the ANC, has left these groups with little hope of
gaining support from the English press. One top UDF official
whom I spoke with contended that, during the 1984–86 uprising,
the entire mainstream press had engaged in drastic and deliberate
underreporting of the extent of rural resistance. "Attracting foreign capital has been the main goal of our local capitalists for the
past one hundred years," he said, "and they are understandably

afraid that if foreign investors see how deep-rooted and permanent resistance really is in this country, well, that will make the
case for sanctions."

Most resistance spokesmen seem to recognize that, while individual reporters may be sympathetic to their cause, they must
contend with editors and subeditors. One official I talked with
even knew enough about newspapers to attribute the UDF's
problems in getting its information and perspective into the *Star*
to a recent influx of conservative editors who arrived after the
government of Zimbabwe took over the Argus paper there.

Qwelane described the paper's editorial structure this way:
"The *Star* is the whole South African situation in microcosm.
The Af. ed. is like a bantustan. Its news editor is like a bantustan
leader. He is black. But he is answerable to another news editor,
who is answerable to a managing editor, who is answerable to the
editor of the daily, who is answerable to the editor-in-chief, all of
whom are white. A bantustan leader is answerable to the Minister of Cooperation and Development, who is answerable to the
Cabinet, which is answerable to P. W. Botha. It's the black local
chief keeping the blacks in order and being answerable to the
white authorities, who are only answerable to other whites."

During the time I was in Johannesburg, one white reporter
had a desk in the *Star*'s undeclared bantustan: a diminutive
young woman with a rooster-tail haircut and a severe manner.
One day while I was talking with Qwelane, she sat, wearing huge
blue plastic earrings and a paisley jacket, eating corn chips, and
staring intently at her monitor. Another young white woman
joined her and together they leafed through the day's editions,
swearing like teamsters over the play their stories were getting. I
had been around for a couple of weeks by then, and I realized
that I had never seen the rooster-tailed reporter speak to any of
her black neighbors, or vice versa—and that these relations were
typical of the social apartheid that prevailed in the newsroom.
Blacks and whites worked with each other as necessary, but they
rarely seemed to hang out together.

The real extent of the gulf between them, though, only dawned
on me when I started asking black reporters if they ever had

white colleagues over to their homes. Not one black reporter had ever had a white co-worker from the *Star* to his house. And only one black reporter had ever been to a white colleague's house— Qwelane, who had once gone to a Christmas party given by Anita Hughes. "Most of these people have never set foot in a township in their lives," one black reporter told me, waving a hand to indicate the newsroom at large.

I recalled a bar in Cape Town that had been a journalists' watering hole. It had been open to whites only, but laws against mixed drinking were being repealed. I wondered if there might be such a place, now integrated, in Johannesburg? According to the blacks at the *Star*, there wasn't. And none of them seemed to regret the fact. Mike Siluma said, "We have far too little in common to want to hang around together." Phil Mtimkulu said, "At this stage, when some things are becoming nonracial, you can become very unhappy about enjoying yourself in these little restricted nonracial venues, because you know you have to return to the stark realities of township life: police vehicles, starving children, untarred roads. It's too false. Also, it's a political problem. You'd rather not be seen lapping it up in Houghton." Houghton is a wealthy white suburb. Montshiwa Moroke, when I asked, just said, "It's an irrational situation. Everything's so abnormal."

Anita Hughes, on the other hand, regretted the social apartheid at the *Star*, particularly when it came to Qwelane. "He cannot escape the fact that, by not being with whites as much as he possibly can, he is developing tunnel vision," she said. "Maybe it would mellow him, and that wouldn't be good. But it would be so good for everyone else. He is so strong-minded."

White reporters on the English-language papers in South Africa tend to be young—the average age at the *Star* is under thirty. The job pays relatively poorly and the raises level off quickly, with the result that those who want to start families move into advertising, public relations, publishing, politics, or some other comparatively lucrative field. As a group, they are anti-apartheid. (I have never met one who was not.) Some are actively sympathetic to the black resistance. Many have done courageous investigative reporting. (There is even a small tradition of white reporters working for the underground. The most recent of these to come to light, a young woman, was on the *Sunday Times* before she left the country, joined the ANC, received military training, returned, bombed several police stations, was captured, and, in December, 1986, sentenced to twenty-five years in prison.)

Still, while talking to white journalists in Johannesburg, I was often struck by the contempt they displayed for their black colleagues. Nearly all of them seemed to say that very few blacks were real professionals—that blacks' regard for facts, their ability to look at the news dispassionately, their command of English were all lacking. Several whites even denied the truth of things I had learned from black reporters about themselves. One woman who had worked with Herbert Mabuza said he had never been detained, much less spent eighteen months in solitary confinement. I inquired whether she had ever asked Mabuza about his experience in 1976. She had not. I told another woman about how Joe Thloloe, when he was detained from 1977 to 1979, only learned upon his release that the black journalists' union of which he was president had been outlawed for over a year. She said, "That's impossible. The guy would have to be just incredibly stupid. Those guys inside know *everything* that goes on." She had, of course, never been arrested herself. Yet another white former colleague said of a black *Star* reporter who is known among his peers for his cool under fire, "I like him, but he's gutless."

Some of this contempt seemed to be reciprocated, although for reasons I found more understandable. One case I often heard cited by black reporters as reason for mistrusting even the most seemingly sympathetic white journalists dated from 1976, when material that black reporters were risking their lives to gather in the townships, and contributing to the *Rand Daily Mail*, was being taken and sold to a British newspaper by a well-known white reporter. It was all material that the *Mail* had decided not to use, but the black reporters, who were mostly stringers, got neither byline nor payment, and they and their brethren have not forgotten.

Most black and white journalists belong to separate unions. This is not necessarily by white journalists' choice; their union is now nonracial. (For many years, it was not, which tainted the organization permanently in the eyes of many blacks. Having their latter-day magnanimity spurned may explain the dynamic that leads to all the sniping among otherwise progressive white journalists at their black colleagues, whose union specifically excludes them.) It was a white *Star* reporter, Sheryl Raine, however, who told me, "It makes perfect sense that we have separate unions. Most white journalists are indifferent to unions. The only time they'll come to a meeting is two weeks before pay talks, when they'll scream that they're underpaid and need more money to buy a Jacuzzi. Blacks, on the other hand, are totally into unions. They understand—and, more than that, they *feel*— the need to organize. And they rightly question the level of militancy among whites. When it comes down to it, blacks will strike and whites won't—it's as simple as that. Whites are afraid of being arrested, for God's sake. Still, I don't think whites would scab again, the way they did in 1980 when the blacks went out for two months and the *Post* was closed and Phil and the others were banned, and all that.

"But the basic issue is commitment. Black reporters see their work as part of the struggle. It keeps them working hours that are absolutely obscene. Herbert once worked for six weeks solid. He was finally *ordered* to take two days off—and he called in on both those days. They are on call at all times—'accessible to the community,' as they say. Meanwhile, the level of commitment among most white reporters is virtually nil. This is a job. When the last edition closes for the day, they're gone."

The longer I spent in the *Star* newsroom, the more it seemed to me that even black and white journalists who were friends saw each other only dimly through the apartheid wall. Thus, when Anita Hughes tried to explain to me why Qwelane preferred to work where he did, she said, "Blacks are funny. You have to earn respect in the black community. And Jon is very highly respected. So no black would move him from a terminal. Over here, he would have to share." Now it's true that there are fewer terminals than reporters in the *Star* newsroom. But nowhere is that truer than in the ghetto—which is why Qwelane can often be found batting out a column across the aisle in the women's page, where terminals are more plentiful. I actually studied this question at close range for some weeks, and concluded that there *is* a pecking order for terminal use in the ghetto. It's an African custom called Whoever Logs On First.

But the most serious failure of communication for black reporters on white papers occurs with the news editors. "Forget the cops," one black reporter told me. "The hardest battle we fight here is with the white editors—to get our copy into the paper. They simply don't trust the stories we bring in, or else they can't handle what people are saying in the townships. They say, 'We can't print that, it's inflammatory.' But that's the *mood*: inflamed."

I recalled how, during Bishop Nkoane's sermon at Margaret Komane's funeral, in Katlehong, Mudini Maivha had been listening intently but taking few notes. Afterward, when I asked why, he said, "It wasn't because what he was saying is not of interest. It's just that it was all too heavy for us to use, too 'hot.' The editors would think it was too heavy for our readers, anyway. Never mind what those *comrades* had to say." (Another reason, I later learned, for not taking too many notes in the field is the danger that the police or the Army may seize the notes and use them to harass activists.) And the UDF press conference at which the vigilante had confessed to killing Margaret Komane— and to being paid by the police to do so—that had also been too hot for the *Star*. Maud Motanyane had covered it, but the editors had not run her story. Instead, they waited to see what other papers—and the police—would do. The *Sowetan* ran the story, but without the man's name and with a bar across his eyes in the photographs. *City Press* ran the story in full the next day, as did the *Weekly Mail*, a sharply edited, independent weekly staffed by former employees of the *Rand Daily Mail*. The *Star* had taken

courage and finally run a story in a late edition, but it was a
wire-service version, shorter and weaker (and less likely to pro-
voke the police) than Motanyane's.

Qwelane was furious about the spiking of Motanyane's story.
Nodding toward the editors' offices across the newsroom, he said
tightly, "I tell you, if I were made editor today, I would fire all
those guys on that news desk. They let their own conservative
feelings cloud their judgment. They just don't believe what we
tell them." That weekend, he devoted "Just Jon" to a redress of
the injury done to Motanyane's story. Drawing on the press-
conference transcripts, Qwelane wrote a dramatic account of
the police payments and fatal firebombings, almost recklessly
risking police reprisal—and editorial rejection—with his tone.
The column ran, but the episode had not been the *Star*'s finest
hour.

"Our editors are still in the Sharpeville era," one white reporter told me, referring to the 1960 police massacre of sixty-nine
unarmed blacks—the incident shook the country deeply and
came to mark the end of one chapter of South African history and
the beginning of another. "They never go to the townships, and
they just cannot believe that the police and the Army *routinely*
murder their opponents now, even little kids. It doesn't seem to
matter how many times their own reporters come and tell them
it's happening. You get the feeling that they lack the most basic
sociological grasp of what South Africa is about today."

The most serious uprising in modern South African history—
it was still going strong in June, 1986—began in the Vaal Triangle, south of Johannesburg, in September, 1984. A white *Star*
reporter who covered it told me, "The only people surprised in
this building when the Vaal Triangle blew were the white sub-
editors who had been relegating all the warnings that they were
getting from the black reporters to Af. ed." The *Star*'s Africa
edition had carried prominent warnings of the approaching confrontation and sent a number of reporters to the Vaal just before
the fighting erupted. "But whites hardly knew that anything was
up. That's why they have this attitude now: 'What did we do
wrong?' "

Chapter 9

At the End of the Day, a Slippered Gentleman

For a sociological grasp that was as up-to-date as modern market research could make it—and for some insight into the departments other than editorial that determine the character of a newspaper—I went to see Keith Holt, the director of advertising at the *Star*. Holt is a tall, red-haired, well-dressed man in his fifties.

"Our strength is retail, and especially classified," Holt told me. "Supermarkets, furniture stores, your larger motor people, banks, and building societies are all very big. We've actually lost thirty percent of classified in this recession, because fifty percent of classified is Help Wanted. But we've been able to counter most of the loss with the Saturday property section. South Africans are like Americans, you see—they move house three or four times in their lives, whereas people in Europe only go once or twice. So, two years ago, we decided to go after the show houses. Traditionally, it was the Sunday papers that carried the property advertising, because people actually *look* at houses on Sunday. But we thought, 'Why not capture them on Saturday, whilst they are still *planning* their weekend?' And it's worked. The property section is up to ninety-six pages."

Holt was so proud of the Saturday property section that I didn't mention some obvious dampening facts about it: that a great deal of the property advertised seemed to be panic selling, a function of "white flight"—four-bedroom houses (plus servants' quarters) in "select neighborhoods" selling for $30,000; that it was only white South Africans who moved 3.5 times per life, everyone else in the country operating within a rather different set of legal and material constraints; that, indeed, all the property advertised in the *Star* was in whites-only areas. Holt must have sensed that my interest was less in marketing as such, anyway, than in how his work reflected the situation in the country as a whole. Unasked, he informed me, "We will not carry any ads that say, 'Whites Only.' In one or two cases, that has cost us advertising. But we just feel that not to do that would be betraying our editorial colleagues, and what the *Star* represents."

Holt's view of the relationship between profit making—which at the *Star* means the advertising department, since it accounts for 80 percent of the paper's income—and editorial content struck me as exemplary. "The *Star* is profitable, and that releases, as I've always said, the editors to get on and do a good job." Holt did make reference, however, to a plan to "slim down" the *Star* that he said would "provide a better ratings structure" as well as "present a new challenge editorially. In the age of television, people haven't got the time to read bulky newspapers. In Europe, the trend toward slimmer papers is well advanced. I don't think it's a knock to editorial to say that we need crisper, better edited stories. Less volume, more quality." Given the volume of the contribution made by advertising to the *Star*'s income, I guessed that Holt would prevail in this matter, although he did say, generously, "I don't foresee the *Star* going tabloid in the next five years."

Holt's remarks recalled points made by Irwin Manoim, co-editor of the *Weekly Mail*, over lunch a few days earlier. "Official censorship is only one of our problems," Manoim said. "There's also the censorship that business and advertising can impose—because the advertising community here just epitomizes white complacency. Advertisers prefer the status quo: a small white minority with a large disposable income, buying things and keeping their noses clean. They see newspapers merely as conduits to customers. They're not just indifferent to a paper's political aims; they're actively hostile. When an issue of the *Weekly Mail* was seized, our advertisers called first thing the next morning, not in support but in *outrage*. They blamed us. 'This is what your irresponsibility has brought!' We're seen as a bad conduit. We're full of doom and gloom. When we asked the management of this restaurant if they would like to advertise in the paper, the owner flipped through an issue and said, '*Ag*, no, there are too many black faces in here.' "

I asked Manoim if that had been a good business decision, if the restaurant we were sitting in would not in fact benefit from advertising in a paper that was obviously widely read in that neighborhood, which was adjacent to Witwatersrand University.

He laughed. "I said they were complacent and conservative, not rational."

When it came to the *Star*, Manoim was scathing. "The *Star* is the South African equivalent of *USA Today*. It is a truly magnificent advertising medium, the perfect reflection of this very gray commercial city. Like any large newspaper, it must aim for the very center of the market, and the center of the market in this country would rather not know what's happening."

In fact, the *Star* aims not for the center of the market, but for its upper strata, as was clarified for me by a promotional film made by the paper's advertising department. The film, which relied on a brusque, technical *Mission: Impossible* lingo and flashy computer graphics, took as its subject "consumer activity" in major metropolitan areas. "Objective: precision geo-segmentation for precision marketplace penetration." South Africa, said the film, because of all its languages, cultures, and economic diversity, was a marketer's nightmare. "Geo-segmentation" involved determining exactly who lived where, and how and when and where they shopped for what. Most "high-potential consumers," it seemed, were found in pockets surrounded by average- or low-potential consumers. "Challenge: to separate the two groups of consumers and exploit the high-potential." The constant danger was "media overspill." For media that extracted the most high-potential consumers from each pocket, with a minimum of overspill, the Argus Company could offer advertisers no fewer than seventy papers to choose from (this figure included many knock-and-drops). Now that was precision penetration.

Keith Holt, too, underlined the *Star*'s special interest in "your A- and B-income readers." He even blamed the death of the *Rand Daily Mail* on that paper's failure to distinguish its target markets. "They had a strong upmarket white readership"—your A and B people—"but most of their readers were actually black. If they had targeted those two markets with two different papers, they would be alive today. But they weren't being honest with advertisers about being a predominantly black-read paper, so the advertisers deserted them." (Irwin Manoim made the same point, though more sharply: "Advertisers closed the *Mail*," he said.) Holt's assessment of the *Star*'s black readers: "We are attracting the thinking black, and possibly the more affluent black." At the same time, Holt seemed to discount the whole geo-segmentation effort when he sighed and said, "En masse, the black is a bigger potential market. It may take four blacks to buy what one white might buy, but at the end of the day you're trying to make money."

I had to wonder if the *Star* was being much more candid than the *Mail* had been with advertisers about who its readers are after Jos Kuper, the *Star*'s market-research director, told me that the *Sunday Star*'s readership was "exclusively white"—that there was no township edition of the *Sunday Star*. In fact, although the circulation of the Africa edition averages only about one-fourth that of the white editions, the *Star* is read by considerably more blacks than whites—and there *is* a township edition of the *Sunday Star*.

But Kuper had other, more informative things to say as well. Though the market-research organization used by the *Star* had stopped interviewing blacks for its annual reports because of "an amazing amount of status overclaiming in the black market—people say, 'Yes, I read *Time* magazine; oh, no, I don't read *Drum*,' when neither statement is true"—she had a plausible explanation for why so many blacks buy the *Citizen*, which has, after all, "a totally wrong editorial profile for the black market. What we discovered was that the big black readership occurred on only two days a week: Wednesdays and Saturdays. The two pre-racing days! You see, the *Citizen* took over a racing-tips section called Gilbey's Punter's Friend from the *Rand Daily Mail* when it closed. Blacks are great punters, and Gilbey's Punter's Friend has lots of credibility with blacks."

As for the blacks who read the *Star*, Kuper shared Keith Holt's view that many of them actually had the "upmarket profile" for which the paper was looking. Indeed, she said, "the better educated blacks read the normal edition—that is, the white edition. Basically, the strategy of the Argus Company is to concentrate circulation in a few upscale markets. It's a narrow and deep philosophy, rather than a broad and shallow one."

Within the confines of this philosophy, the *Star* was in an enviable position, since, according to Kuper, 73 percent of all A-income whites in the Johannesburg area read the paper. This monopoly of the most coveted market would seem to give the paper more freedom to take editorial chances than it would have were it faced with real competition. But then there is the *Citizen*, which, although a morning paper and distinctly downmarket, is also a tabloid ("and people love tabloid," according to Kuper, because "it's such an easy read"), and actually provides some competition for circulation—not to mention the irritation of its constant suggestions that the *Star* and other liberal papers are unpatriotic. It is the *Citizen*, along with television, that Keith Holt is watching when he advocates a "slimming down" of the *Star*. The *Star*, one realizes, could be shifted a long way in the direction of the *Citizen*, both in design and editorial content, without losing its upscale readers, who have, afer all, nowhere else to go.

Allister Sparks, the former editor of the *Rand Daily Mail*, believes that mainstream South African papers like the *Star* are "dinosaurs," that they are moving too slowly to keep up with the times and will eventually be as obsolete as the newspapers that once catered to white colonials in Northern Rhodesia were in Zambia after independence. Gavin Stewart, who heads the department of journalism at Rhodes University—the only university journalism department in South Africa—disagrees. He thinks that the big papers "will survive indefinitely, even if they become nothing but big spongecakes. There is a market for all that advertising, it sustains itself economically, and there will always be hacks around who can fill in the spaces between ads with whatever dribbles out of Pretoria." The transition to spongecake-hood is already well advanced, according to Stewart. Few of the graduates from his department go to work at newspapers anymore—they go into advertising or broadcasting instead.

Hal Miller, the executive chairman of the Anglo American Corporation, while discussing in the *Star* the economic problems of South African newspapers, offered a rosier view of the future. "I have a picture in mind of the year 2000, where we find a slippered gentleman sitting in his study with a good cigar and a good brandy—browsing through his newspaper. Electronics don't allow browsing, which makes newspapers unique."

This sort of British-inflected vision of prosperous gentility seems to suffuse the *Weltanschauung* of the *Star*'s owners and management. Keith Holt, who worked for years in London and wears immaculately cut blue suits, absolutely exhaled it when we spoke. And it percolates down through the ranks in different forms. In that pub I knew in Cape Town, where white journalists gathered to hoist pints of bitter and toss darts, the badinage round the bar might have been imported fresh from Fleet Street. Few, if any, of the reporters who drank there ever went, on assignment or otherwise, to the Cape Flats—the bleak backyard of that beautiful city, where most of the area's inhabitants live in a vast archipelago of ragged townships and squatters' camps. But it is the anger in those townships that will shape South Africa's future. No, the slippered gentleman in his study, with his good cigar and his good brandy, lives in Cloud Cuckoo Land. In the year 2000, it is far more likely that South Africa will resemble the blasted, beleaguered, war-torn land of J. M. Coetzee's *Life and Times of Michael K*, in which half the country is interned in camps, and all information is twisted and scarce.

Chapter 10

"We Are Black
Before We Are
Journalists"

That paper's irrelevant.' That's all you hear when you identify yourself as a *Star* reporter in the townships," Maud Motanyane told me. "People are far more critical of the press now than they ever were before." Community papers, church and union newsletters (which number in the hundreds), even clandestine pamphlets and tracts—almost anything produced outside the white power structure—are more highly regarded, she said.

Phil Mtimkulu, who worked for years on a Soweto community newspaper, agreed, but registered a professional demurrer. "People *like* the community papers, but they don't *buy* them," he said. "They like to read the truth. They like stories that say the cops shot school kids when the cops shot school kids, and they don't want an overemphasis on official comment. But the papers that they *buy* are those that carry football and overseas news. If there is a big disaster in New Mexico, they want to know about it. And the *Star* is No. 1 for giving people news from all over the world. Of course, it may not please those who want a vehicle for the liberation struggle. We're always hearing, in social situations, that we're not being radical enough."

Indeed, there seems to be bitter agreement in black South

Africa that the white papers don't take many risks in their opposition to the government—the way Anthony Heard, the *Cape Times* editor, did in 1985, when he published an interview with Oliver Tambo, the president of the African National Congress, for which he was immediately charged with quoting a banned person. The failure of the white press to convey even the outlines of the political debates going on inside the resistance—despite the fact that since 1976 the center of gravity in South African politics has clearly shifted from the white arena to the black—is another point one hears made repeatedly by blacks, who believe, not without reason, that the outcome of those debates will crucially affect the country's future, and whose own lives are, in any case, already being shaped by their fury and complexity.

But the difficulties of reporting on the resistance, a task that falls largely to black reporters, are daunting. Besides the danger of aiding the security forces in their harassment of their opponents—of providing what the black community considers "classified information"—the sensitivity of the resistance organizations to criticism is such that any black reporter who engages in it is likely to be accused of "assisting the system." And there is no shorter route to oblivion than that in black South Africa today. Moreover, every black reporter is in constant danger of becoming identified with one camp or another in the power struggles that rage inside the resistance.

The two main tendencies can be characterized as charterist and noncharterist. The charterists, who subscribe to the Freedom Charter, a broad statement of political goals and beliefs that was formally adopted by the ANC in 1956, are represented by the United Democratic Front aboveground and by the ANC underground and in exile. The leading noncharterist groups are the Azanian People's Organization, aboveground (Azania is their name for South Africa), and the Pan-Africanist Congress (PAC), a breakaway element of the ANC, which was also outlawed in 1960 and also took up armed struggle, but has fared relatively poorly in exile and underground.

The political orientation of AZAPO can be traced to the Black Consciousness movement, which arose in the late 1960s and flourished in the early 1970s before it was crushed by the state in 1977. Some Black Consciousness activists went on to found AZAPO. The pivotal event in the recent history of South African resistance, however, was the launching—by a broad coalition of democratic forces, including former Black Consciousness activists—of the UDF in 1983. The UDF quickly became the largest aboveground resistance organization in South African history.

The political differences between the charterists and their opponents are slight—on paper. Both seek to replace white-minority rule with a nonracial democracy. Their main difference has to do with the issue of white participation in the liberation struggle. The charterists welcome whites; noncharterists argue that progressive whites should work in their own communities—that when they belong to organizations with blacks they dilute black determination and, because of their training and resources, nearly always take leading roles, so that the organizations merely reproduce the apartheid society. This was the epochal insight of the Black Consciousness movement, and for that reason noncharterists today are still often called "BC." While the difference might seem no more than a tactical one, it encompasses the most emotional issues in South Africa, along with political antagonisms whose roots are often a generation or more deep.

AZAPO is a relatively small organization, lacking the mass base of the UDF, but its following among black students, professionals, and intellectuals is significant. AZAPO and the UDF are both officially committed to nonviolent tactics, but their members are invariably caught up in the violence of township politics. In fact, the mayhem they were visiting upon each other while I was in South Africa was frightening. Although the charges were almost surely unfounded, the warring factions often accused one another of "selling out" and of working with the police. Jon Qwelane described the situation as "just a raw power struggle." (One American correspondent I know said, "It's the Sharks versus the Jets," and much of the fighting did seem to be over turf. In Soweto, every neighborhood was faction-identified: AZAPO controlled Orlando East; Diepkloof was UDF territory.) Bishop Tutu, recalling Moses' return from the mountain to find the golden calf, told me, "Even when people are striving for their liberation, you never find unanimity." The UDF-AZAPO struggle reached into every corner of township life. Because black politics does not involve voting, and the townships have so few resources, the political organizations—or "orgs," as everyone calls them—necessarily concentrate on controlling those resources. Funerals, football teams—even kindergartens—become the political battlefields. And at street level the UDF-AZAPO fighting often seemed to lack any ideological content.

It did not lack for mortal dangers to black journalists who became identified with either faction, however. "The leaders may still be willing to talk to you—they want their story in," Mike Siluma told me. "But the activists don't care about that. If they know you're affiliated with their opponents, they may just take you out." Qwelane had faced this problem, particularly after he dared to criticize the Freedom Charter in a 1985 column; he had since had to go out of his way to cover the UDF favorably and extensively, and was still widely thought of as pro-AZAPO.

The *Sowetan* had the same problem, on a larger scale. An editor there told me that the paper was not anti-UDF but the rumor that it was somehow got started, and became impossible to stop. The editor partly blamed the paper's competitors, *City Press* and *New Nation*, for the *Sowetan*'s problems. Both had obvious reasons for wanting to see the *Sowetan* discredited, and both were strongly pro-UDF. He also imagined the ANC leadership in Lusaka noticing that, "while the UDF has been getting a lot of very good publicity abroad, there is a black paper in Johannesburg that does not seem to be beating the drum sufficiently. So they come and look into our staff and find ex-PAC guys, ex–Black Consciousness guys, who are quite powerful, who can't be swayed, and who are quite powerful in MWASA" (Media Workers' Association of South Africa, the black journalists' union). The UDF-affiliated Congress of South African Trade Unions considered calling a boycott of the *Sowetan* and, although no boycott was called, some local activists enforced one anyway, with the result that the *Sowetan* was not being sold in some major Rand townships, including Alexandra and Tembisa, because of the danger to its distributors. *Sowetan* reporters had been barred from UDF meetings and funerals.

UDF leaders soon realized that the situation was getting out of hand—even members of UDF-affiliated unions were being attacked as they tried to deliver papers—and the cooler heads among them tried to call off the vendetta. But, according to the *Sowetan* editor, "They've created their own little monsters, who say, '*Sowetan* is against the comrades,' or '*Sowetan* sends our photos to the police'—all these crazy things they just make up. So we're having a hell of a time. Not with sales—our circulation is pretty comfortable. But with fear for our lives. Our staff is really in danger." The *Sowetan*'s editors had made concessions to the UDF leaders, such as agreeing to shift their labor reporter to another beat, but at the time I talked to them they had not noticed any lightening of the pressure. "These guys want to be the only bull in the kraal," was the best explanation that one of the editors could offer. And, in a dark moment: "When they come to power, I just think they'll put the whole *Sowetan* staff against the wall and shoot them."

Lest it seem that only one faction threatens journalists, let me hasten to mention that I once spent an evening with a black journalist who was a former AZAPO official but was believed to have "gone over to the other side," the UDF. He was in hiding at the time—staying illegally in a white suburb—after hearing that he was on a hit list maintained by an AZAPO student group in Soweto that is known for its ferocity toward "traitors." His wife and children were hiding somewhere in the countryside. He was still working as a reporter, but only in certain townships and neighborhoods—and the fear that poured off him, even on that easygoing evening in white Johannesburg, was absolutely palpable. This man was not a police informer, not a collaborator. He was a dedicated opposition journalist. His politics never even seemed to me to be particularly pro-UDF.

Most of the pressure that the "orgs" put on black journalists is less deadly than this, and it is worth recalling that it is different not in kind but only in degree from what has gone on between reporters and community groups in South Africa for decades.

Interest groups lobbying journalists, for that matter, is universal. Still, the situation in which I found Mudini Maivha one afternoon in the newsroom struck me as peculiarly South African. He was sitting at his desk staring at a crumpled scrap of paper. I asked him what was up. "This young kid just came in here, telling me he was from the Vosloorus Civic Association," he said. "They've decided to call a consumer boycott and a rent boycott. This is their press statement. They want it released. But I've never heard of this group, so I made some phone calls, and discovered that the Vosloorus Civic Association closed up shop in 1983. So I asked him a few questions. Now, it seems the meeting at which these resolutions were made was attended by a total of three people. This boy has no mandate. So I told him, 'You want me to help you impose these boycotts that the people of Vosloorus have not decided on. I won't do it.' After that, he threatened to denounce me as anti-UDF. I suppose this is really just a power play—to start a new Vosloorus Civic that will be automatically affiliated with the UDF. But that is how these organizations are now. If you make any investigation of their claims, they say, 'You are anti-us.' And we must take their threats seriously." Maivha peered unhappily at the scribbled "press statement." That evening, he said, he and some friends were scheduled to meet with some Soweto comrades about their threats against a journalist who had estimated the crowd at Diliza Matshoba's funeral at five thousand. It seemed that the comrades thought the crowd was larger. Maivha heaved a huge sigh, and said, "I suppose we must just put away our notebooks and come with pangas and kill each other!"

In addition to overzealous comrades, there is, as Qwelane puts it, "a lawless element that preys on the struggle, especially now, when unemployment is so high and everybody is always looking for an angle." These are the "hoodlums"—the *tsotsis,* as they are called in the townships (the word comes from "zoot suit")—whom the government has traditionally blamed for even the most clearly political violent black protest. In the present chaos, the tactics of criminals are sometimes spectacular in their cynicism. *Tsotsis* posing as comrades will go from house to house at night announcing a transport boycott, and then, when people are trudging across the fields to work the next morning, they mug whole neighborhoods. *Tsotsis* often participate in attacks on township liquor stores. In black South Africa, liquor outlets are symbols of "the system," and torching them is a resistance ritual, but looting the stores before burning them down and selling the liquor for personal gain erases the political significance of such attacks. This kind of opportunism is not regarded kindly by the comrades. Indeed, impersonating an activist is considered a capital offense by many activists. While I was in South Africa, five "fake comrades" accused of running an extortion ring in Port Elizabeth were summarily burned to death by the real thing.

This is all part of the "black-on-black violence" so often announced, at times it seems contentedly, by Pretoria. The death toll attributed to it was in fact running several times that attributed directly to the security forces during the time I was in South Africa. Most of the killing, however, was being done not by the comrades but by right-wing vigilantes, who have often been linked to the police. The composition of vigilante groups varies from place to place, but it usually springs, as in KwaNdebele, from some combination of local businessmen (shopowners, shebeen keepers, taxi owners), civil servants, and policemen—those with a vested interest in the local status quo—and the mass of unemployed, uneducated men, most of them from rural areas, who can be induced or, if necessary, coerced to fight the comrades. Once the battle in a given area has been joined, it often develops a blood-feud momentum of its own, but the political lines usually remain relatively clear. In the province of Natal, where fighting between vigilantes and comrades has been particularly intense, the vigilantes are nearly always linked to Chief Gatsha Buthelezi's paramilitary Zulu "cultural organization" Inkatha, which is, on its turf, the most feared group in black South Africa. (In early June, 1986, at least one Inkatha leader was actually boasting to the newspapers about all the "enemies"—by whom he meant UDF supporters—the group looked forward to killing.)

The first journalist to be killed in action in the 1984–86 uprising (excluding Montsho Lucky Kutumela, of the *Lebowa*

Times, who died in a Lebowa jail cell in April, 1986, shortly after being arrested) was, not surprisingly, hacked to death by right-wing vigilantes. George De'Ath, a thirty-four-year-old white South African freelance cameraman working for British television, was covering the fighting between comrades and vigilantes near the Crossroads squatter camp, outside Cape Town, in early June of 1986. When his sound man mistakenly addressed a group of vigilantes as *qabane*—"comrades"—they attacked the newsmen with pangas and axes, fatally wounding De'Ath.

The vigilantes have nothing to gain from cooperating with any journalists except those of the government press, which has become increasingly open in its support of their rampages. *Beeld*, for instance, recently editorialized, "Nobody can get a firmer grip on Black intimidators than their Black fellow-countrymen." Though many of them are illiterate, the vigilantes have come to understand that black journalists or foreign journalists—any journalists who are not with the security forces—are unlikely to report anything favorable to them. (Reporters from the government press enter the townships *only* under the protection of the police or the Army. In early 1986 in Kagiso, Jon Qwelane actually saw two journalists from SABC riding inside a Casspir with weapons in their hands; the reporter had a shotgun, the cameraman a gun used for firing tear gas.) The vigilantes often have a great deal to hide: violent crimes, police payoffs. In most cases, they lack even a coherent leadership with any political case to make. (While I was around, a large number of vigilante groups were calling themselves "The A Team," after the American television series.) For reporters, the vigilantes have definitely become the most dangerous faction of all.

But the vigilantes are a recent addition to the picture in the townships, and in most places represent no significant fraction of popular opinion. Indeed, popular opinion has been moving rapidly leftward for many years in black South Africa, and when black journalists refer to "the community," they mean the vast majority that wants to see an end to white-minority rule.

Black journalists talk constantly, in fact, about their "responsibility to the community." And that responsibility is often conceived in opposition to—or, at least, in competition with—professional responsibility. Maud Motanyane, who was thinking at the time of leaving the *Star*, told me, "Even with the nine years that I've worked here, I don't feel a part of this establishment. I never could. Instead of having a commitment to my employer, I have a commitment to my community. I do a story because I see something that should be exposed rather than because I see that it would be a good story for the *Star*."

Qwelane echoed her feelings. "We started saying it in the seventies, and it is truer now than ever: We are black before we are journalists. Facts are sacred—we certainly have no need to exaggerate the situation—but the only journalism worth doing in our situation is crusading journalism, work that will help to advance our struggle." In 1980, Zwelakhe Sisulu, the editor of *New Nation*, framed the imperative in a much-quoted address to a national congress of MWASA, of which he was then president. "In our situation, the question is not whether one is a propagandist or not, but whether one is a collaborationist propagandist or a revolutionary propagandist," Sisulu said. "Because we have expressed a desire for radical change in the scheme of things, we must be propagandists for change. It has been said that there are no politics of neutrality in this country and conversely there cannot be a journalism of neutrality. We accept that the press has to be responsible, but responsibility of the press in this context merely means co-option—that the press must not interrupt social coherence at the expense of political fulfillment."

Rex Gibson provided me an inadvertent glimpse of the gulf that separates white editors and black reporters in this area when he described, with evident satisfaction, a recent meeting with his black reporters in which they had reaffirmed their commitment to "professional neutrality." I asked some of the black reporters on the *Star* about the meeting. None of them seemed to know what I was talking about. Finally, Phil Mtimkulu said, "Oh, that meeting when Gibson talked to us about objectivity. Yes." As it happened, I had already heard virtually every one of the black reporters make scathing remarks about objectivity in journalism. "Objectivity means reality as the editors see it," one said. "They'll tell you the glass is half-full when what *we* experience is that it is half-empty." Approaching the subject from a different angle, an editor at *New Nation* told me, "The best thing about being on a black paper is not having to hear all that talk about objectivity."

A related benefit of being on a paper openly committed to the liberation struggle, he might have added, is the extra access that reporters are afforded to some sources in the townships. *New Nation*, in particular, is so closely tied to the UDF that it is often the first paper to hear of developments within the resistance. Of course, the paper's ability to report critically—or, in some cases, even accurately—on the UDF is correspondingly compromised. The more partisan elements of the black press, because of their clear attachment to a political program and drive for power, are sometimes compared, in fact, to the Afrikaans press prior to 1948. (The comparison could be physical as well. Reporters at the *Sowetan*, who work on vintage manual typewriters, call their office "The Newspaper Museum of South Africa," and the facilities at *City Press* and *New Nation* are no better.)

The tension between journalism and activism felt by black reporters sometimes blows a fuse. When Bokwe Mafuna, who now lives in exile in Paris, was covering a Black Consciousness movement student conference in the northern Transvaal in 1972 for the *Rand Daily Mail*, the conference organizers warned journalists that anyone who referred to them in their stories as "Non-Whites" would be ejected. All references in Mafuna's copy to "blacks" were changed at the *Mail* to "Non-Whites," and he was duly thrown out. Mafuna quit his job on the spot. He drove the newspaper's car back to Johannesburg, followed by conference delegates in another car, and then returned with them to the conference as a delegate. Thereafter, he became a full-time activist.

Jon Qwelane, for his part, claims to shun politics. Speaking of his mother, he once told me, "She leaves politics to politicians and thinks I should do the same, which I'm trying to do. I have no political ambitions whatsoever." After a moment, he added, "But that doesn't mean I can't question what's going on around me." And it doesn't mean that he doesn't have political views.

"Because I'm a journalist, I don't belong to any political organization. But we can't help having our allegiances. Remember, white journalists can vote. We can't vote." Qwelane's allegiances emerge clearly in his conversation. I've heard him declare, on being pressed, "I believe irrevocably in African nationalism," and, on another occasion, "I believe in an Africanist Azania." Statements like these place Qwelane firmly in the noncharterist camp of the resistance. His own history illuminates his orientation: his father was a supporter of the PAC, and Qwelane grew up politically in the mid-1970s, the heyday of Black Consciousness. On the key tactical question that divides the resistance, Qwelane echoed Steve Biko, the preeminent theorist of Black Consciousness, when he said to me, "I simply can't belong to the same political organization as whites. All they will do is dilute my efforts toward my own self-determination. This is not reverse racism. We can make common cause. But the struggle in South Africa really cannot be fought nonracially. Black kids are dying. White kids are not dying."

A surprising number of black journalists take the noncharterist line: surprising when one considers how the noncharterist organizations have been dwarfed, and in many areas marginalized, by the mass popularity of the UDF. I've heard various explanations for this state of affairs. Bishop Tutu told me, "Black Consciousness is a very cerebral thing. You need to be very smart to see that being pro-black is not the same thing as being anti-white. So that has made BC always somewhat élitist in its appeal." A *Sowetan* editor said the opposite: "Black Consciousness speaks directly to the feelings of the people. A lot of comrades who claim to be UDF/ANC actually speak a Black Consciousness language." Phil Mtimkulu traced the politics of many black journalists to their formative years in the BC era, and to their frustration with the then closed white journalists' union, which led to the founding of a BC-oriented black journalists' union. MWASA remains, at least in the Transvaal, BC-oriented. Ameen Akhalwaya, who worked on the *Rand Daily Mail*, cited the bad experiences that most black journalists have had with white editors and what he called "the whole forked-tongue liberalism." And it does seem that black journalists, particularly those on white papers, cannot help retaining a highly developed awareness of just how different—qualitatively different, *structurally* different—their opposition to apartheid is from that of even the most sympathetic whites. Blacks who work in less-constant proximity, or in a less-complex relation, to white colleagues, or at less-intellectual jobs—which is to say, the vast majority of blacks—may find it easier to believe in the efficacy of a "nonracial" approach to the freedom struggle.

And yet, paradoxically, Qwelane's relations with some of his white colleagues are exceptionally warm. A *Star* photographer, white, once helped me out of a financial jam (I was sugar-free in a downtown parking garage), and when I told Qwelane about it, he chuckled and said, "Garth is a star. A superstar. Any time of the day. I tell you, *any time of the day*."

The fact is that Qwelane's politics are thoroughly idiosyncratic—even riddled with contradictions. He once defined for me the fundamental problems of liberation as "one, repossessing the land, and, two, self-determination for the African masses." By "repossessing the land," he said, he meant nationalizing agriculture. As for "the African masses," he said, "Everyone who owes allegiance to Africa will be African, regardless of race, creed, or color." On other occasions, however, I heard him talk about white South Africans as if they were foreign interlopers: "Would the French or the Germans let the Americans come in and take over their country and treat it as if it were their own? No, they would throw them out if they possibly could." And, when I later asked him how he saw the nationalization of agriculture, he said, "The farmers will still own the land, but the majority of the people will control it." Qwelane describes himself as a socialist, yet he seems uninterested in the elaborate ultra-leftism that characterizes most AZAPO spokesmen. (AZAPO is, on the whole, to the left of the UDF, and even of the ANC, despite the ANC's close alliance with the South African Communist Party.) At the same time, he is a Catholic and pledges allegiance to the current, conservative Pope. "The Pope is my spiritual leader," he told me one night as we sped down the highway after a long day's reporting. "His infallibility is part of our dogma, and, no matter what happens, I will die a Catholic."

What all this rather splendid ideological inconsistency amounts to, of course, is simply the politics of a natural-born writer. Qwelane is not fond of political rhetoric, not really comfortable with it (I have heard him described as having "a superficial analysis"); he clearly prefers more concrete language, a discourse of details and narrative. He tries to inhabit that unaffiliated territory in which a distinctive voice can be heard, an individual view developed. Like any good writer, he tries to call them as he sees them. But the situation in South Africa affords a black writer little, if any, space for such "personalism"—even stylistically.

I was struck by the response I got from a young white leftist when I told her, in answer to a question about what I was doing in South Africa, that I was, among other things, spending time with Qwelane. We were standing around a sizzling barbecue on a sun-splashed lawn in a white suburb at the time, and she said, with some surprise, "But he's so bourgeois." I knew exactly what she meant. Qwelane's writing, both in his columns and in his features, conveys a sensuality, a materialism, an implicit conviction that what most people really want in life is to be able to stand around a sizzling barbecue with friends on a peaceful rolling lawn in the sunshine. This is quite out of keeping with the austere and astringent vision that prevails increasingly in the resistance. The pressure to be grimly militant operates on all black journalists— I often thought I saw it working on the gang at the *Star*—though it flows more from their sense of responsibility to the black cause, of course, than from the expectations of white radicals.

But this pressure can make calling them as one sees them, according to one's own values, problematic, to say the least. For instance, deploring in print some act of putatively revolutionary violence because it seems cruel or wanton or wrong may very well play as "reactionary" in the townships ("The comrades accuse us of 'coming with niceties,' " Qwelane told me), and so destroy a writer's reputation—even propel him into the outer darkness reserved for "counter-revolutionaries." Every black field reporter has seen terrible things. Maud Motanyane once witnessed, at very close range, the necklacing of a young woman accused of being a police informer. When she told me about it, a year later, her voice fell into a pained monotone. The worst part, she said, was the smell of burning flesh. It seemed to permeate her clothes. She could not sleep for days after the incident, and she still could not forget the smell. She had rushed back to the newsroom from the scene and knocked out a story on deadline, but her byline was not printed—partly because what she wrote made it clear that she was skeptical about the murdered woman's having been an informer. At one time or another, most black reporters have seen the brutal enforcement of boycotts by young activists: old women found with goods bought in defiance of a consumer boycott being forced to drink cooking oil or eat laundry soap. Most black reporters have seen angry crowds on the warpath. How to write about "the community" then?

"Ungovernability" has been a strategic concept in ANC policy statements for many years; after the most recent uprising began, in September, 1984, it became a grassroots political rallying cry. And it was in the areas where black journalists primarily work— the townships—that the goal of making the country ungovern- able had been most nearly reached. This, of course, was what made their jobs so dangerous. And yet I heard more than one black journalist proclaim ungovernability to be a good and wor- thy resistance strategy, "considering the alternatives available to us." At the same time, it was clearly very difficult to write— particularly for a white-owned, white-read newspaper—about a chaotic situation, about violence in which the political content may even be negligible (mob rule, old scores being bloodily settled), in a way that did not at least imply disapproval of the forces of lawlessness. This was the minefield that Qwelane con- fronted in Uitenhage, and that black journalists confront in all their coverage of unrest. The pressure on them not to offend the comrades or the "orgs" is immense. Qwelane says, "We are trying to do a good job in a bad time, but the truth is we are all thoroughly intimidated." (By mid-1986, there were calls coming from resistance leaders for the transformation of ungovernability into "people's power," in which democratic organizations would fill the power vacuum.)

These dire tensions undoubtedly help fuel the resentment of black reporters against the editing that their copy receives. "When we are witnesses to police excesses, and the community knows what we have seen, we are expected to come back here and fulfill our role," Qwelane said. "Then, when our stories are questioned, and not printed, or the police version of events is given prominence, our credibility is devastated." Qwelane told me about an incident in Katlehong—a police attack on a funeral in which one person was killed and fourteen were injured. He saw the whole thing, even managed to get the names of all the victims, and wrote the story. But it appeared alongside a police version of the same incident, in which a mob was stoning a liquor store, tear gas was used, and no one was injured. "The people of Katlehong were furious," Qwelane said quietly. "If we don't emphatically expose what everyone knows these guys are doing, how can we expect the people to trust us?"

Stories that come from sources are at least as chancy as eyewitness reports. Mike Siluma explained, "People give you information because they think it's important. But if it comes out on page twenty, because that's where the chief subeditor decided to put it, the people think you're not taking them seriously. They don't understand what happens here. So you're in constant danger of being attacked in the townships for what your newspaper does." Against attacks that may become more than verbal, there is almost nothing reporters can do. Police protection is not an option, Siluma said. "That would be the kiss of death."

Besides all this extraordinary stress—being caught, as Rex Gibson puts it, "between the hammer and the anvil," trying to maintain some degree of intellectual and professional independence in a time of mass revolutionary action—black reporters must try to conserve their integrity in conventional ways. I once overheard Alf Kumalo, the *Star*'s senior black photographer, invite Qwelane to a soccer match for which he had been given tickets by a bank executive. Qwelane sighed, then said, "No, thanks. I don't like to be in anybody's debt. Next time, if he embezzles funds, I can't write the story."

The most remarkable thing, for my money, about the black reporters I came to know in Johannesburg was simply their continuing outrage. They understand only too well that the maintenance of white-minority rule requires endless brutality, and yet they seemed shocked and infuriated by each new instance of official violence. Qwelane told me, "If an activist's house gets attacked by police, people just say, 'Well, that's the system.' But the police *shouldn't* be doing that. We *can't* just take it for granted." The values that underlie this outrage may or may not be "bourgeois," but they surely fly in the face of the revolutionary's cold-eyed understanding of class struggle. They peel back, too, some of the hard-bitten cynicism for which newspaper reporters, especially those who cover the activities of the police, are everywhere known. These values also fly in the face of the idea, long held as gospel throughout the resistance, that South African society is totally and terminally "abnormal." Instead, they assume a social fabric, a social contract, that includes due process and fundamental decency. This can seem, under the apartheid circumstances, wildly naïve, but the fact is that black journalists are in this respect only typical of black South Africans.

Most blacks with any degree of political awareness probably agree with the basic characterization of the English-language press as a "veneer of democracy" which only helps legitimize the system. Certainly mainstream opposition papers, like the *Star*, seem to provide many white readers with not so much hard news or clear understanding as with the illusion of an open society— an illusion that few blacks share. Blacks know that the real problem is not the authorities' breaking the laws but the laws themselves. The South African state is, as someone recently wrote of the KGB, "utterly repressive even when it operates in a perfectly legal way. . . . A squeaky-clean KGB would leave the Soviet Union a perfect police machine." And yet blacks buy the white liberal newspapers, and they read them not just for the football results and the international news but for the political news, the latest "unrest" details. And they shake their heads, cluck their tongues, and murmur, "Shame!" over the unending reports of repression and massacre.

What this suggests is that at least an *idea* of normality, of a civil society, is really too profound for most people to discard wholesale. A clear comprehension of the state's fundamental illegitimacy, even an ardent belief in the need for a revolution, may form the basis of some conscious attitudes, but it gets left out of others. Journalists know that the problem is, at bottom, the country's laws, and yet they struggle endlessly to expose the government's violations of those laws. And this is how the South African revolution proceeds. There are a few trained guerrillas inside the country, who embody an opposition to the system that is absolute and, in that sense, simple, but most of the millions of South Africans who are fighting to overthrow the government have jobs, rents, mortgages, families. They live and function in society, and their relationship to it, psychological as well as material, is inescapably complex. To reject it utterly, at all points and all times, would be not just terrifying but impossible.

The role of black journalists is, in its ambiguity, paradigmatic. And the fact is that in the black community the standing of reporters remains generally high. Qwelane's face has become well known since his photograph began running next to his byline on "Just Jon." As a result, strangers are constantly offering him lifts when they see him at the side of the road (they call him by name: "Come on, Jon, get in"), or dragging him into shebeens (where he orders Cokes), eager to know the man who speaks so candidly for the black man in the street. The same thing happens to Alf Kumalo. He has worked in journalism since the 1950s, and his face—salt-and-pepper mustache, big, gentle eyes, shining brown pate—was featured for years in a magazine advertisement for a photography school. Walking with Alf in Soweto is like walking with Keith Hernandez in Manhattan.

All this may change, of course. Already, one hears young activists referred to as "the Year Zero children," after Pol Pot's fanatical child fighters in Cambodia. And a mentality reminiscent of the Khmer Rouge does reveal itself in the mutterings of some comrades against blacks whom they consider "middle-class," and thus inherently counter-revolutionary. If this kind of lumpen Maoism ever becomes widespread, black journalists will be in an even trickier position, for they are exceptionally well educated and well paid by the standards of black South Africa. "As it stands," Phil Mtimkulu told me, "so long as you live in Soweto, and you drink in the shebeen, your kids go to the local schools, and you identify with the people's problems, people don't resent you. If you're up in the clouds, of course, they may begin to resent you."

None of the black reporters I came to know seemed up in the clouds as they dashed around the Witwatersrand, dodging bullets, inhaling tear gas, and trying to get the goods on the government. But the space for vigorous reporting is constantly narrowing, and I was curious what journalists, blacks and whites, thought about the prospects for a free and independent press in a future South Africa—in, specifically, a black-ruled South Africa.

Asking around produced a stark pattern of response. Whites, even strong supporters of the UDF, were pessimistic. Pat Sidley, the head of the white journalists' union, told me, "The idea of a free press has hardly penetrated the black community here. The government has seen to that." Others, making the same point, tended to blame, besides the government, the press itself—for alienating blacks with racist, condescending Africa editions, for failing to defy the government sufficiently, for failing to publish enough of the truth, and failing to really support the freedom struggle. Denis Beckett, the editor of a non-aligned magazine called *Frontline* (and *not* a UDF supporter: "There are a lot of tuppeny Hitlers running around in the UDF," Beckett told me), said ruefully, "Our South African idea of freedom is the freedom to shut down the other fellow's freedom." Gavin Stewart, the professor of journalism, pictured a historical pendulum, "and pendulums don't stop in the middle, unless they've been swinging for a very long time. The perception inside the resistance will probably be that the press was not fair before the revolution, and there will be a getting-even process."

Most black journalists, on the other hand, seemed truly optimistic. Joe Thloloe, despite the forebodings of some of his colleagues at the *Sowetan* about what the ANC may do with them after the revolution, claimed not to be worried about the outlook for newspapers in a majority-ruled South Africa. "As the struggle intensifies, people will see the need for full information, for a reliable press, for something wider than mere propaganda sheets," he said to me. "It's all part of the growing pains." Oliver Tambo recently assured the world that there would be a free press in an ANC-ruled South Africa—which would make the country highly unusual in present-day Africa. But Zwelakhe Sisulu perhaps suggested a more accurate picture of such a future when he told me, "If you take the right stance now, and side with the people in their liberation struggle, you will be in a strong position afterward. We will be able to point to our record and demand our rights as a free press in a liberated South Africa."

In the meantime, black journalists live in apartheid South Africa, where they are very often, as Qwelane says, blacks before they are journalists. A story that Qwelane told one night while he and Mudini Maivha and I were driving to Soweto brought this point home to me. I had asked Qwelane if he had ever been shot. "Ye-e-e-es," he said. To my surprise, Maivha had never heard the story.

"It was in 1977, in a Portuguese shop, in Doornfontein," Qwelane said. Doornfontein is an old, white, working-class neighborhood in Johannesburg. "I went in there with a friend of mine to buy cigarettes. The shopkeeper didn't give me the correct change, but when I pointed that out, he went crazy. He hit me on the head with a basting spoon, opening quite a big cut, and then he grabbed my friend and started choking him. The next thing we knew, he had pulled out a pistol. At that point, we ran for the door, But he chased us down the street, shooting at us, and he hit me in the thigh, shattering the bone. Then he and his brother dragged me back to the shop and, I tell you, they really beat me up well. They were dropping crates full of soft drinks on my chest! I really thought they were going to kill me."

Qwelane paused to light a cigarette, then went on.

"Finally, the cops got there—my friend had called them. I was losing consciousness by then, but I could hear them telling the cops all sorts of rubbish—that I had come in there with a gang of seven guys and tried to rob them, that sort of thing. And I could see that they were showing the cops a gun that was not the gun he had shot me with. They had stashed the first gun up on a high shelf. I just managed to tell the cops about it, telling them to look up on the shelf, while I could still speak. And they looked up there, and found the gun. You see, it was unlicensed. And the other one was licensed. So the guy was arrested after all."

Qwelane laughed with satisfaction. "I spent about a month in hospital. First they removed the bullet, then they put a big steel pin inside the bone. My leg stayed numb for quite a long time, and I once heard the doctors discussing amputation. My God, that was terrible. But finally the leg began to regain some feeling. The therapy went on for months and months, and I never thought I was going to walk properly again.

"When I got out of hospital, I brought charges against the guy who shot me, of course, and then, suddenly, all these other cases came to the surface. It turned out that the same shopkeepers had simply shot another black man dead, and had blinded an old black woman by throwing hot chili sauce in her face. Nothing was ever done about these other cases, until we ran a couple of stories in the paper, and the relatives decided to take action. Unfortunately, before any of the cases were heard, those shop-keepers disappeared. They just closed up their place and left. They probably went back to Portugal. But now, you know, I'll go a long way out of my way to avoid patronizing a Portuguese shop."

"Or a Greek shop," Maivha said. "Or an Italian shop."

"You just never know what will happen in there."

"It's always over change," Maivha said. "They try to cheat you, and when you say something, they go completely crazy. They're worse than the worst Afrikaners."

Qwelane laughed. "And I never even got my cigarettes!"

Chapter 11

Abiding the Umlungu

My ability to observe black reporters going about their work was limited. My company slowed them down. Worse, it endangered them. Above all, my presence distorted situations—at times to comic effect. Once, Mudini Maivha and Herbert Mabuza were trying to talk their way into a hospital to interview a shooting victim. It was a hospital for blacks, but the head of hospital security was a young, quite dense white guy, and he insisted on dealing with me, rather than with Maivha or Mabuza. The only problem was that I never said a word, so he wasn't sure whether I spoke English or Afrikaans. He kept switching back and forth between the two, addressing me half the time as "sir," half the time as "*meneer*," and all the while regarding me, as Mabuza later put it, "like a puzzled puppy." It was uncomfortable and embarrassing, and we never did get into the hospital, but Maivha and Mabuza laughed about it afterward, and Mabuza later cracked up the reporters in the ghetto with a wonderful imitation of the guard. What I had really wanted, of course, was to see what would have happened at the hospital if I hadn't been there.

The situation made me grateful for night assignments, when much of the unwelcome attention we got in the townships because of my being along disappeared. Under cover of darkness, I could feel invisible as we bumped along through the acrid waves of coal smoke, past the endless little houses with their windows lit yellow by kerosene lamps, asking directions of the dark shapes in the street. I remember one night in Mamelodi, a huge township near Pretoria, looking for a house where a man and his sister had been murdered. Our search took us to a series of parties where *mbaqanga* bands played in the yards, people danced and laughed, and the smell of roasting meat overcame the coal smoke. The murdered man had been a bantustan politician, but he was from far-off KaNgwane, on the Swaziland border, and his death seemed to have little local political significance. The people at the parties were also involved in bantustan administration, which helped explain the conventional gaiety of the parties—a gaiety quite out of keeping with the prevailing atmosphere in South African urban townships. It was almost possible, that night in Mamelodi, to imagine we were covering the news in any Third World country, where the mixture of poverty and politics, custom and conflict, remained at a bearable temperature, a temperature far below that of black South Africa. This got harder to do when we finally found the dead man's house and were sitting in the bedroom with his three daughters, photographing bullet fragments they had pried from the walls and realizing that the shootings had been not the result of some rural feud but a professional assassination, carried out with an AK-47, probably by the ANC. In fact, the political atmosphere in Mamelodi had been deadly since the day, a few months earlier, when security forces unaccountably opened fire on a crowd composed largely of elderly women who were marching, with police permission, to the local administration office to protest the continued presence of troops in the townships. At least thirteen people had been killed, and many more maimed or wounded.

One thing that I could see, easily and always, while hanging around with the *Star*'s black reporters, was the truth of Sheryl Raine's comments about their commitment to their work. In the late afternoon, long after the last edition had closed, when the newsroom at large was silent and empty, the ghetto still buzzed with activity: telephones ringing, keyboards clacking, terminals glowing, people talking in half a dozen languages, reporters coming and going. When things finally did slow down, people often lingered, waiting for that last source or interviewee to call, or for somebody to return from the field so that they might travel home to Soweto together. The unwinding that did not happen at any Johannesburg pub would take place then, as the reporters relaxed, joked, told stories.

One day, Maud Motanyane recalled a funeral in Tembisa that she went to cover with Alf Kumalo and a reporter from the East Rand bureau. A child had been killed. The press was barred from the township, so the three of them went in on foot. They reached the house of mourning, and while they were inside interviewing the bereaved family the police barged in. "I just grabbed a blanket and pulled it around me, pretending to be a mourner," Motanyane said. "We all pretended to be family members. But then I looked down and realized that I was wearing *red boots*. What a dreadful color to wear to a funeral! The cops were demanding to see the mother of the child who had been killed. They were trying to force the family to bury their child on that day. But the grandmother took over, and she was wonderful. She told them that her daughter had left. 'She disappeared when you teargassed the house at night,' she said. 'And we will not bury this child until she returns.' The cops didn't know what to do with her. Finally, they just left, without saying a word to us. But I tell you, I haven't worn those boots to work again."

Motanyane, red boots or not, is exceptionally good-looking— so much so that, when she took a break from journalism in the late 1970s and worked for a while in public relations at Barclays Bank, her face was featured in the bank's advertising. And yet, as the only black reporter on the *Star*'s white editions, the most polished appearance sometimes availed her little. When she went to cover the meetings of the Johannesburg City Council, for instance, she was often, she told me, mistaken for the maid. In fact, Motanyane trained both as a librarian (at the University of Zululand) and a journalist (through the Argus Company's "cadet" program), and spent a year on a scholarship in the United

States. She has a droll, feminist wit, and when she was not "out hunting news," as she and her colleagues say, she was a leading light in the *Star* ghetto during the time I was around. Once, when I mentioned to Qwelane how much I liked Maud, he gazed across the newsroom in her direction for a minute, then abruptly said, with immense feeling, "Maud is a *sparkler*." Qwelane and Motanyane have been friends for ten years, and his feelings are obviously reciprocated—which did not keep her from saying to me, on another occasion, with a slow, fond laugh, "Jon's such a snob. And he actually used to be *worse*. If he saw me opening a dictionary, he would say, 'Ask me, babe. I have all the answers.' He still looks at the way some of these other fellows dress, in their lumberjackets, and he just can't believe it, even though they're his friends."

On another day, Alf Kumalo—whom his colleagues, in honor of his age, sometimes call *baba* (at other times, in honor of his bald head, they call him "Old Hardtop")—was telling a story that took place in Swaziland, a small neighbor of South Africa's whose leaders are understandably secretive about the "security agreements" into which they have been forced by Pretoria. The moral of Kumalo's story, which emerged after a series of slapstick episodes involving the Swazi police, concerned the wisdom of wearing a traditional loose African shirt with big waist-level pockets in front: "Because that shirt can really come in handy. When the cops demand your film, you just brace your camera against your belly, and start fumbling all around to remove the film. If you're clever, you should be able to drop the exposed roll into your pocket, and snatch out a blank one. That's what I did with those Swazi cops, and they never suspected a thing. I gave them the blank film, they released me, and I got out of there. I just hope they never saw the pictures we printed."

Kumalo's listeners cackled approvingly. Outfoxing the police, even if they aren't South African, is the Lord's work. The occasion for Kumalo's telling this story was an incident a few days before. He, Qwelane, and I had attended a meeting—billed as a "tea party," to avoid a ban on meetings—of the Detainees' Parents Support Committee in a church basement in downtown

Johannesburg. Several hundred people, many of them sad-faced mothers and grandmothers, had been there. They were addressed by a young white human-rights lawyer, who apprised them of their rights—"virtually none," he said, if they could not find out where their loved ones were being held—in a crisp, angry speech that was simultaneously translated into South Sotho by a young black woman. When Kumalo and Qwelane left the church to get their story in, Qwelane spotted a car parked across the street with two white men inside it. "Those are cops," he said. He pointed them out to Kumalo, and one of the policemen immediately jumped from the car and started toward them. Qwelane and Kumalo ran down an alley, with the cop in pursuit, and into the lobby of the Johannesburg Sun, a busy new international hotel. Kumalo quickly unloaded his camera and passed off the film to a young white reporter who happened to be in the hotel lobby. He and Qwelane assumed that it was the film the police wanted.

"They want to know who was at the meeting," Qwelane explained to me later. "If they get the film, they can take it and develop it and identify one of the people in the crowd from their files, or from their familiarity with activists. Then they go find him, and they beat him up until he names some of the other people in the photos. Then they go to them, beat them up, and get some more names, and in this way they make a sweep. If they can do it from our photos, they don't have to bother with infiltrating the meeting themselves and trying to photograph everyone there, or with the bad publicity they get if they raid the meeting with all those foreign film crews there. This way, it's all done at night, in the ghetto. We must be careful about which photos we print, for reasons that are obvious, but we must also be careful about what happens to the pictures we take and don't print. That's why the comrades are so sensitive about having their pictures taken at all."

Qwelane and Kumalo waited in the hotel lobby, and the policeman loitered outside, obviously reluctant to pursue them in front of the many tourists and foreign businessmen present. Eventually, with the film long since delivered to the *Star*, the cop gave up. But the police did not abandon their stakeout. About an hour later, two blocks from the church, where the "tea party" was still in progress, I was in a car with Qwelane, stopped at a light, when he said, without looking up from the cigarette he was lighting. "That's a cop." He nodded, almost imperceptibly, toward a muscle-bound young white man, wearing jeans and a denim jacket, who was lounging against a nearby wall and staring fixedly back at the church. "He's been there for two hours. He hasn't moved a muscle. Look, he doesn't even notice those two pretty girls walking past. That bulge in his jacket is a two-way radio. The shorter bulge on the other side is a gun."

The stoplight changed.

I accelerated.

Qwelane chuckled. "Ye-e-e-e-es," he said.

If it seems remarkable that the *Star*'s black reporters were willing to take me with them into the field, that is because it was remarkable. It didn't happen right away. I spent hours hanging out with them in the newsroom first. The fact that I had lived in South Africa before made a difference—my incessant questions would have been even more abecedarian if I had not—but their willingness to help me arose finally, I think, from the fact that they were journalists themselves. They were used to relying on the kindness of subjects and sources.

Some of the reporters were easier for me to get to know than others. With Mudini Maivha, for instance, I discovered that I needed to disassociate myself from his one previous experience of Americans. It seemed that he had recently taken a journalism course, taught by an American professor, through an exchange program. Afterward, Maivha told me in a bitter voice, the professor had gone back to the United States, where he announced that his students—all of whom were black journalists—supported Reagan Administration policy toward South Africa. This untruth had apparently caused Maivha and his classmates a lot of trouble. (It had also caused the professor trouble. Although there was some doubt about whether he had actually made the offending statements, MWASA had responded with a boycott of

American exchange programs.) Maivha told me this story only after I mentioned that I had written critically about United States policy toward South Africa, and when it became clear that we agreed on the subject, he seemed relieved. We were talking in the newsroom at the time. Maivha stood and said he was going to get something to eat. He tentatively invited me along.

"I'm just going for some pap," he said.

I went with him. Behind the *Star* offices, adjacent to the main embarkation area for "non-white" buses to Soweto and the West Rand, there was a small African and Indian shopping district. Maivha led me there—to a crowded little café where African workers ate mealie pap and braised meat from paper packets. We bought packets of tough, spicy steak and pap, and we carried them back to the newsroom, where Maivha, with obvious amusement, watched me eat the greasy African workingman's lunch with my fingers.

Phil Mtimkulu was a more complex proposition. In fact, our relations were difficult from the start. Mtimkulu had been my contact at the *Star*—a friend in Cape Town had put me onto him. I first phoned him from the United States and, though he seemed a little harried, he said O.K., he was willing to let me shadow one of his reporters. Beyond that, I didn't really expect him to go. He didn't know me from a bar of soap. He would certainly need to see who I was before he would know if he really wanted me around. I wanted at least a reporter's name, though, and Mtimkulu, after some prodding, gave me two: Rich Mkhondo and Chris More. On the basis of our five-minute telephone conversation, I flew off to South Africa.

But when I called Mtimkulu on my second morning in Johannesburg, he sounded surprised to hear I was there. I asked him when I could come by. He said, "Later sometime. We're on deadline just now."

I gave him a couple of hours, then went down to the *Star*. After talking my way past a security guard (a dim-looking, heavily-sideburned white guy whom several black men seemed to be having somewhat less luck in passing), I took the elevator to the third floor. A receptionist (white, female) phoned Mtimkulu to say I was there. Several minutes later, Phil appeared, wearing a cardigan sweater and regarding me dubiously. He directed me to a couch in the elevator foyer. He seemed nervous, and while we sat there making conversation he never once looked me in the eye. Several times he jumped up and went back into the newsroom, leaving me alone. I noticed a sign over the newsroom entrance: "NO UNAUTHORIZED PERSONS ALLOWED."

It was the same message I was getting from Mtimkulu. After having me refresh his memory about what I wanted to do, he told me that Rich Mkhondo and Chris More had both left the *Star* in the weeks since we had spoken on the phone. In fact, Mkhondo, the reporter whom I had thought sounded perfect for this story, was presently working in Philadelphia, Mtimkulu said. (I thought I detected a suggestion that I might have saved a lot of trouble and money by simply going to Philadelphia.) As for my accompanying black reporters into the field, well, that would present problems. I couldn't go in one of the *Star*'s cars with them. Their work was dangerous enough already. So I would have to go in my own car. And I would have to hire a driver who knew the townships; I would never be able to keep up if I drove myself, or know how to evade trouble. I would also have to stay in a downtown hotel near the newsroom, so that I could be ready to go out on a story at a moment's notice. Even then, we would have to see what the editors, and the reporters themselves, thought.

During one of the intervals in this disastrous interview, while Mtimkulu was away in the newsroom, I listened to a young, white, preppy type tease a blonde woman in her thirties as they waited for an elevator.

"So where's your husband?" he asked.

"Lusaka," she said.

"What's he doing there?"

"Talking to the ANC." She pronounced it "ank," a little affectation I had not heard before. "They invited him up."

"So where's his copy?"

"He's filing lots of stories!"

"I've only seen one little thing."

"You should start reading the paper!"

The young man grew serious. "How's it going?"

"Fine," said the woman, and added wryly, "Come the revolution, *we'll* be O.K."

Elevator doors opened, the banterers disappeared, and I was left wishing passionately that I had come down here to work with such glib, accessible people, rather than with the strange, evasive, uneasy Mtimkulu, who obviously wished I would just go away.

I didn't oblige him, though, and after an hour or so he got exasperated and took me on into the newsroom to meet Ron Anderson. Mtimkulu seemed amused when I later started hanging around the ghetto without official permission, but he still seemed to keep his distance from me. He liked to complain that my interviews with him were a burden, though they rarely lasted more than a few minutes before we were interrupted, and I was actually less interested in formal interviews than he seemed to think I should be. He liked to complain so much that I decided he secretly looked forward to our sessions. And it was during one of them that things between us turned the corner.

At my suggestion, we had repaired to a bar near the *Star*. It was a big, new, brightly lit place, and, though Mtimkulu muttered something about the bar's possibly being whites-only, and he seemed uncomfortable at first, we managed to get served, and, after a couple of beers, were deep in conversation. I was interested in the impact that the Black Consciousness movement had had on black journalists. "It had a very big impact," Mtimkulu said, and his tone grew urgent. "Everybody needed Black Consciousness—as a foundation for self-confidence. I mean, look at me. I have two university degrees, and some white man who has never even finished high school will assume he can intimidate me, simply because I am black. And if I don't have self-confidence, he *will* intimidate me. That is simply the nature of this society."

I suddenly found myself unable to look at Mtimkulu—even though he had, at least rhetorically, ordered me to do so, and he, for a change, was looking at me. Instead, I stared out the window beside our table (it was raining, and night was falling, and I could see past the *Star* offices into the bus-stop district, where African herbalists sold roots and potions in crowded little shops) and wondered at what it must have taken for Mtimkulu, who was so "black" in manner and appearance, to have risen to the position he had in the white-dominated world of Johannesburg journalism. As far as I could tell, he behaved very differently around whites—with far greater reserve—than he did around other blacks. And yet the amount of "self-confidence" that he had amassed, his success at the *Star*, seemed extraordinary. His new openness with me was both welcome and unnerving. Later, on a visit to his house in Diepkloof, Soweto, I was disconcerted by the sight of a well-thumbed book titled *How to Overcome Nervous Tension and Speak Well in Public*.

That visit to Mtimkulu's house was the last stop on an impromptu tour of Soweto that started one afternoon when Phil asked if I wanted to go along on an errand to the outskirts of the township. We ran the errand, and then he asked if I would like to see the house to which he had been confined for three years under his banning order—it was nearby. We went and had a look at the house, which turned out to be a tiny tarpaper bungalow at the edge of a field. "And I wasn't even allowed to cross this road here," Mtimkulu said, indicating the road we were looking across. "Even though the shebeen was here, on this side!"

I thought that called for a drink, and Mtimkulu agreed. The shebeen in question, a cozy old house with dark-green walls and ancient Coca-Cola posters on the walls, was quiet at that hour, but the shebeen keeper was amusing and the beer was cold, and by the time we rolled back out on the road it was late afternoon and Mtimkulu was determined to show me the sights of Soweto. Which was how I came to see: Bishop Tutu's house; Winnie Mandela's house; Morris Isaacson High School (where many of the leaders of the 1976 uprising had been students); Tshabalala's Shacks (a terrible tin-shack city built and operated by the "mayor" of, and most corrupt businessman in, Soweto); Regina Mundi Cathedral; Jabulani Stadium; the precise burned spot in

the road where a bus carrying supporters of Chief Gatsha Buthelezi had been firebombed a few days before; and Mtimkulu's
new house—a scantily furnished, brand-new ranch-style house
facing, across a small valley, rows and rows of primitive "hostels"
where thousands of mineworkers live.

Of the black reporters on the *Star,* Jon Qwelane was for me
both the most approachable—it was, after all, his generous,
why-not attitude that got me over the hump to begin with—and
the most problematic. Qwelane was willing to talk for hours on
end, and he always had something to say, but, like Mtimkulu, he
also usually had a number of breaking stories on his mind, which
often gave him an abstracted air. After a few weeks, too, the
sheer amount of time that we were spending together seemed to
begin to unsettle him. Once we were talking in the newsroom and
somebody asked Qwelane something about his background, and
I heard him answer, "Don't ask me, ask Bill. He knows much
more about me by now than I know about myself."

The situation came to a head one day when I mentioned, quite
casually, to Qwelane that I thought the story I was there reporting might turn out to be a profile of him. He blanched. "A
profile? You never said anything about wanting to write a profile.
If you want to write a profile of someone, you should write one
of Joe Thloloe. Joe is someone who has earned that kind of thing.
I haven't."

Qwelane paused, and I found myself wondering how much of
his distress at my announcement (which was really less an announcement than a passing notion) was genuine modesty and
how much of it actually flowed from the social and political
climate in black South Africa—a climate which, for reasons
having to do with both the liberation struggle and African tradition, strongly discourages self-aggrandizement, or any sort of
grandstanding, particularly among younger people and those
who may have suffered less, in relation to older people and those
who may have suffered more. I knew enough, in any case, to
have anticipated Qwelane's reaction, so I was irritated with myself, and I didn't know what to say. But Qwelane wasn't finished.

"I don't know, man," he said. "I feel like you're always there, watching my every wrong step. It's like being followed by the police."

These were wounding words, under the police-state circumstances, and before I could reply Qwelane was called away. And that turned out to be the last time we spoke that afternoon. I was miserable afterward, although, brooding on his remarks, I decided that I sympathized completely with him. I only had to imagine the tables turned: how would I like somebody following me around, asking me endless questions, carefully noting my every tic and foible? "Oh, you're wearing your yellow socks today. Are those the ones with a hole in the toe?" Every profile subject had to put up with it, but it was worse somehow doing it to a fellow writer. Writers are used to making up their own stories, used to selecting which parts of their lives to make public—not to having the selection made for them.

That evening, while I was stewing by the fire in the big chilly house where I was staying, Qwelane phoned. I didn't remember having given him the number there, so I was surprised—I was also delighted—to hear his voice. He said he wanted to apologize for his reaction that afternoon; I had caught him unawares, that was all. I stammered something about how he had not been in the wrong, and how I wasn't really thinking seriously about writing a profile of him, anyway. He gave a rasping laugh. "Good," he said. "Then see you in the morning, old chap."

Chapter 12

State of Emergency

Dates, commemorations, provide a focus for a mass political movement, a pivot on which events may turn. Since 1976, the single most charged date on the South African resistance calendar has been June 16, the day that Soweto schoolchildren marched to protest their inferior education, the police opened fire on the marchers, and the ten-month national uprising known simply as Soweto began. Vigils, marches, strikes, riots, and fierce repression have marked the day every year since. In 1980, when I was teaching in Cape Town, we managed to keep the school where I taught open through two months of the students' boycotting their lessons, but on June 16 the school was closed, fighting broke out, and over the next two days dozens of people were killed by police. In 1986, the tenth anniversary of the Soweto uprising promised to be an unprecedented confrontation.

During the first week of June, the government announced a ban on all commemorations of the date, but the UDF, AZAPO, and the black trade unions continued to call for a general strike, Bishop Tutu and others urged churches to defy the ban, and investors showed their foreboding in the form of a slide in the value of the rand below the psychologically important plateau of forty American cents. Only three months before, a seven-month limited state of emergency had been lifted. Just the same, journalists and activists began to look for a preemptive blow from the government. Percy Qoboza, the editor of *City Press,* who was once jailed for five months without charges after the authorities closed another paper he edited, told me on June 3, "All people who are opposed to this government are busy packing their pajamas."

Nine days later, P. W. Botha informed Parliament that "the Government possesses intelligence regarding plans which have been made by radical and revolutionary elements for the coming days," and a nationwide state of emergency was declared, featuring drastic new restrictions on the press, sweeping new powers for the security forces, and the arbitrary imprisonment of thousands.

Jon Qwelane went to work before dawn on June 12, running down a tip about raids on the homes of community leaders in the West Rand. Finding that most of his contacts in the area had disappeared, he decided that the story couldn't wait till Sunday, and phoned the *Star* newsroom to give it to the daily. "The first thing they said was, 'Is it more detentions?' That was when I knew," he told me later. The state of emergency was announced at noon, twelve hours after it had gone into force. When I heard the news and called Qwelane, the first thing he said was "These guys never learn."

That afternoon, as the long and growing list of suspected detainees was pouring off the wire in the newsroom—the late final had run a preliminary list of several hundred names—the phone rang, Qwelane answered, and I watched him start scribbling. What he wrote was: "13(D) of Emergency Regulations effectively prohibits publication of names or identification of anyone detained or arrested in terms of emergency regulations or in terms of Public Safety Act of 1953, without official permission." It seemed that the emergency regulations had just been published in the Government Gazette. At her terminal in the ghetto, the young white reporter with the rooster-tail haircut was toiling over the *Star*'s swelling list of the disappeared, eliminating repetitions, correcting misspellings, punch-drunk and giggling after several hours at the task. Qwelane relayed the news he had just received. She stared at him, seeming not to comprehend. "But we *should* publish the names," she said.

"That's the spirit," Qwelane said wearily.

She went back to work.

"It never rains," Qwelane muttered. "It never rains."

Alf Kumalo, Herbert Mabuza, Mudini Maivha, Montshiwa Moroke, and Phil Mtimkulu were scanning the long sheets of computer paper coming off the wire. There were students, teachers, priests, professors, trade unionists, community leaders, white anti-conscription activists, even the elderly mother of an executed guerrilla—it was unhinging to think of all the brutality and terror represented by that spidery, alphabetized readout. And the black reporters knew personally a great many of the people who had been picked up. They whistled, muttered curses, and shook their heads: "Look, they got the whole *family*." There were nervous jokes about which one of them would go first. "See you in Sun City," Mabuza kept saying, meaning Johannesburg Prison. Qwelane, meanwhile, had gone to work on a new Sunday column. The one he had already filed was obviously obsolete now.

Then word came down from the news desk of the *Sunday Star*—this was Thursday—that the editors wanted a lead story under the head "BLACK LEADERS APPEAL FOR CALM." Qwelane went into a fast burn. "That's an insult," he said. "That's kicking a man when he's down." He waved a hand angrily toward the cascading list of detainees. "How are we supposed to preach peace when we are under this kind of attack? How do they think *we* feel on a day like this? I won't do it." Qwelane grabbed a ringing phone, listened for a moment, suddenly stopped glowering, broke into a rich laugh, and said, "Hey, bo. What emergency?" But when he hung up he looked upset again. He stood, wrapped a long blue muffler around his throat, and murmured to me, "I've got to meet someone who's on the run. If Phil asks, I went to the library to get a book and I'll be right back."

A call came from the daily news desk for Mtimkulu. He scribbled some notes, hung up, and turned to his reporters. They were still studying the list of detainees, which was now being yanked from all future editions, in accordance with the newly published regulations. Mtimkulu announced, with scorching dryness, "They want the shebeen reaction to the state of emergency."

No one said anything.

Mtimkulu waited a beat. "O.K., I'll do it myself."

As he collected his things, I asked him how he would approach the story. He sighed. "I'll be subtle," he said. "I'll go to a shebeen where they don't know me, order a beer, and say, 'Hey, what's been happening today?' People will say, 'Oh, England won.' They'll just talk about soccer. Maybe they'll get around to the state of emergency, maybe they won't. I can't bring it up, though, just like that—people would suspect I was an informer. But really, this is the kind of story you can write in bed at home."

Mtimkulu left for Soweto. The other reporters hung around. It was the first time I had seen them, either as individuals or as a group, look aimless. The state of emergency seemed to have sent some of them into shock. Their beats, the stories they lived for, a major portion of South African reality, had just been erased by a stroke of some white politician's pen. Many of their friends and nearly all their contacts were suddenly in jail or in hiding. The rest of the newsroom was emptying out, the day's work done. In the sports department, across the low partition, two old racing writers tapped out their pipes, straightened the stacks of Transvaal Computaform racing forms, packed their briefcases, and departed. It was as if the only part of the newsroom shivering under the chill of the emergency was the ghetto.

The regulations outlawed the filming or photographing of the security forces in action or of "any public disturbance, disorder, riot, public violence, strike or boycott, or any damaging of any property, or any assault on or killing of a person." They also outlawed the printing of any "subversive statement," for which they provided an extremely broad definition. It included any statement "calculated to have the effect or . . . likely to have the effect . . . of inciting the public . . . to resist or oppose the Government"—such as a call to strike, demonstrate, question conscription, "take part in . . . any boycott action," support disinvestment or sanctions, or practice civil disobedience—and any statement that might conceivably weaken "the confidence of the public . . . in the termination of the state of emergency" or promote "any object of any organization which has, under any law, been declared to be an unlawful organization." Since a large number of outlawed organizations had among their goals a democratic South Africa, it was now apparently illegal even to "utter," much less publish, possess, display, or disseminate, statements advocating democracy.

Under the emergency, press coverage of unrest would be effectively restricted to items released by a newly established Bureau of Information, in Pretoria, all of whose "information" would first be vetted by the security forces. The security forces themselves—the police, the Army, railway police, and prison officers, collectively referred to in the regulations as "the Force"—were indemnified against all civil and criminal liability arising from their actions. And this was perhaps the heart of the matter. Police and Army beatings, killings, arrests, torture were now beyond the purview of the courts (let alone of the press). The security forces were empowered to close businesses, impose curfews, and seal off areas to nonresidents—and one of the first areas to be sealed off was Soweto. There were provisions for the seizure of publications, and page after page of regulations concerning detainees.

It was decreed that, without the specific authorization of the Police Commissioner, detainees could not have visitors, write or receive letters, or be given bedding or food parcels. The only reading matter they would be allowed was "the Bible or any other Holy book of religion." A long list of "disciplinary contraventions" for detainees was published, setting punishments for such offenses as singing, whistling, being a nuisance, causing discontent among fellow prisoners, being insolent or disrespectful toward a member of "the Force," and giving false replies under interrogation—punishments that included fines, "strokes," solitary confinement, and "dietary punishment." What legalistic compulsion drove the regime to publish these jailhouse details? Perhaps it was simply a desire to suggest that rules obtained inside the prisons—that the widely held suspicion that the real situation inside them was one of sadistic mayhem was a slander perpetrated by revolutionaries and their allies in the press. In any event, those voices were now silenced. Even the names of detainees had become "subversive statements."

The short-term purpose of the crackdown was clearly to prevent a general insurrection on June 16. The government was also hoping to check the rise of the white parties on its right, which had been getting great political mileage out of charges that the Botha government was soft on black dissent. The long-term goal, which became more and more obvious as the number of detentions rose—to ten thousand, then, as the months passed, to twenty thousand—was to break the momentum that black resistance had gained over the previous two or three years. The main targets were the township "civic associations," which had become the "alternative structures" in many areas where the government-created council system had been destroyed. "Civics" affiliated to the UDF were being hit especially hard. The UDF itself was difficult to ban, since it had a loose, decentralized structure, but its local and national leadership could certainly be neutralized, and many of its alternative structures destroyed, by a prolonged siege of police terror. Of course, none of this was new in South Africa, except in degree and in details.

What was new about the 1986 emergency were the unprecedented restrictions on the press, both local and foreign. The government's claim that it permitted "the freest press in Africa" had been decisively forfeited. In fact, the Foreign Correspondents' Association of South Africa announced that its members were "now subject to probably the most severe censorship applied to foreign journalists anywhere in the world."

The Afrikaans press applauded the imposition of the state of emergency. *Die Vaderland*: "It is our opinion that the announcement of a state of emergency is not only justified by the expected events, but is in fact essential." *Die Burger*: "When large-scale unrest, supported by sabotage and terrorism, is organised, no government may neglect to take precautions against it. That is why many people were taken into custody country-wide." A cartoon in *Beeld* showed beefy arms labeled "Emergency Powers" lighting a lamp of "Order" in a night of "Violence." Several Nationalist editors alleged that the emergency had been, as *Beeld* put it, "declared chiefly to protect Black moderates from Black radicals," having been, in the words of *Die Volksblad,* "necessitated by barbaric acts such as 'necklaces' of burning tyres, people buried alive, 'people's courts' and other forms of intimidation."

At the same time, the government press showed an understanding of black life that roughly corresponded to the number of black reporters it employed. *Die Transvaler,* for instance, observed, "The emergency measures will not make a jot of difference in the daily lives of law-abiding South Africans." *Die Transvaler* was apparently unaware of such inconveniences as the Army roadblocks that had been thrown up around many townships, including Soweto, where the interrogations and vehicle searches were causing huge traffic backups, making even law-abiding people hours late for work.

In its role as cheerleader for the emergency, the government press was evidently excused from observing all the fine points of the new regulations. Thus, *Rapport* on June 15 ran a banner page-one headline, "SA MUST BURN," and followed it with what was perhaps the most inflammatory lead ever published in a South African newspaper: "South Africa must burn. The Union Buildings [the South African equivalent of the United States Capitol] must burn. Seats of government throughout the country must burn. White residential areas must burn. Tomorrow, June 16th, will be the beginning of the final onslaught against white South Africa—an onslaught which will reach its climax on December 16th, which will become known as Freedom Day." In another context, these might have been construed as subversive statements. They were presented so dramatically here, of course, only to impress upon readers the "evil plan of the ANC" that had necessitated the emergency. Alongside this story ran a large color photograph of a white soldier crouching to talk to a small black boy in a township near Pretoria, with the caption "PEACEFUL."

This was the tune being played incessantly by the Bureau for Information, and enthusiastically echoed by the government press: that the emergency had proved an instant success in curtailing violence. The only reservations that government papers expressed about the emergency concerned some of the press restrictions. These reservations were modest, normally confining themselves to a hope that the measures would be necessary only temporarily, and would not tarnish the country's reputation overseas for having a free and independent press. The unbridled behavior of the English press was frequently blamed for having brought these curbs down on innocent heads.

Within the confines of the new regulations, the opposition press denounced the emergency. The *Star*'s editorial on the day after the announcement described it as "an admission of the National Party's failure to maintain government within the bounds of an already eroded Rule of Law. . . . There were other options open to level-headed rulers, from negotiations to declaring [June 16] a public holiday, but the course chosen was that of an arrogant, frightened and misguided government." The editor of the *Sowetan* simply called on the government to quit: "They have been doing this for years and matters have not worked themselves out. The people of this country have had enough. Enough of apartheid. Enough of this Government." Opposition editors warned readers that their papers were being censored— stories in the *Star* on sensitive subjects carried at the bottom a large "X" beside the message "Report Restricted"—and emphasized the point that the most damaging censorship was self-censorship, which, they said, was being widely practiced.

Not so widely practiced that the June 13 issues of the *Sowetan* and *Weekly Mail* were spared banning, however. That afternoon, security police conducted a massive swoop on newsstands, street vendors, and shops, seizing all copies of both newspapers for apparent violations of the new regulations. The *Sowetan* had published a list of some two thousand suspected detainees, along with the famous photograph (long considered, though never formally declared, illegal) of the body of Hector Petersen. The *Weekly Mail* had dared to suggest that the government was taking the country "down a road to nowhere," which was apparently construed as weakening public confidence in the idea that the emergency would end someday. The seizures were every journalist's nightmare (and every newspaper owner's—they were very costly), and the effect, as intended, was to further inhibit reporting. As one *Sowetan* columnist wrote, "Before, the Press had been going along like a haltered horse, but it has now been reduced to a muzzled watchdog which can only make a muffled growl."

Some of the growling still contained a sense of gallows humor. On June 14, Rex Gibson wrote, "If you get detained, remember it is also an offence to sing and whistle in your solitary cell. Of course, you may find it a relatively easy temptation to resist." David Anderson, the *Sunday Star* cartoonist, drew P. W. Botha, accompanied by a hulking goon with the face of Louis Le Grange, the Minister of Law and Order, coming upon a beggar with a sign "Blind Deaf and Dumb," pointing, and saying, "A potential journalist." In another Anderson cartoon, a bound figure completely wrapped in bandages and labeled "Press" sits under a police interrogation lamp. Botha stands glaring at the figure, his fists balled, and says to the Le Grange goon, "Tell him to stop breathing so loud."

Opposition papers took to leaving blank spaces in the middle of stories to indicate censored material. One *Star* headline, "SOMETHING HAPPENS AT RESIDENCE," was followed by the lead "Something happened at the University of the Witwatersrand residence in Soweto in the early hours of Sunday morning," followed by a blank space. (The unreported event was a police raid and the detention of a large number of students and teachers.) But the Minister of Law and Order soon decided that blank spaces were "subversive," whereupon the *Sowetan* announced, "We will now fill the spaces with the most innocuous of writings." Mock-serious essays about potatoes and about petty disputes in the bantustan assemblies followed.

Actual censorship was largely in the hands of a paper's lawyers. I was sitting in the *Sowetan*'s offices when the text for a leader-page piece about South Africa's three states of emergency (1960, 1985, 1986) came back from the Argus Company lawyers with fifty percent of the copy excised. The editor I was talking to looked over the story, shaking his head sadly. "And this is such an innocent piece," he said. "It just compares the different regulations. We'll have to use pictures to fill all this space." On another day, I was getting in an elevator, leaving the *Star,* when Peter Sullivan, an assistant editor and columnist, burst out of the newsroom and thrust a sheaf of paper through the closing elevator doors into my hands, saying, "Take this back to America with you. The lawyers just killed it." It was a column considering the question of whether South Africa could be accurately described as a police state.

The vagueness of the restrictions on the press was deliberate. It kept reporters, editors, and their lawyers unsure, defensive, aware that any number of things they were already publishing could suddenly be deemed violations. David Steward, the director of the Bureau for Information, routinely threatened journalists at the bureau's briefings with punishment for contraventions, but refused to clarify the rules, blandly suggesting that they retain lawyers to advise them. Once he had suggested it, Steward actually seemed to relish this idea. "I think the legal profession is in for a lot of business, and the longer they mull over it, the more money they will make," he said.

The Bureau for Information's daily briefings were presided over by Steward, an ex-diplomat, whom one Johannesburg columnist described as "a man with a face like virgin newsprint," and Leon Mellett, a sullen character who held the rank of brigadier in the South African police but was previously known mainly for his work as a leading man in the romance and adventure "photo comics" popular among South African schoolchildren and semiliterates. The briefings were not distinguished by their informativeness. They were held in a large paneled, chandeliered room in the Union Buildings—an imposing Italianate complex, designed by Sir Herbert Baker, overlooking the sleepy white suburbs of Pretoria. The first day's session produced the news that eight people had been killed in unrest the previous day, one by security forces, the others in "black-on-black violence." No details were offered—not the names of the victims, the circumstances of their deaths, not even what parts of the country the killings had occurred in. The press was simply expected to publish this "information." As Steward said, "You can take it or leave it."

The Bureau for Information declined to answer many questions, or to confirm or deny some of the myriad rumors now swirling through the blacked-out country—one reporter was even forbidden to report her own question. Relations between the bureau and much of the press were soon openly antagonistic and, less than a week after it was established, the bureau decided that it would only address questions submitted in writing at least four hours before its briefings. It then moved the hour of its briefings back to 3 P.M.—too late for the afternoon papers' deadlines, as the *Star* pointed out, but ideal for government television news. The Nationalist press did not appear to mind the new arrangements; the *Citizen* observed that "the Bureau should not have to put up with obstreperous media men."

It has long been alleged by the South African government that many of its problems, both internal and external, are the fault of the foreign media, whose coverage of the country has been "biased," and in the crackdown of June, 1986, foreign correspondents were a primary target. On the day the emergency was announced, crews filming interviews on the streets of Johannesburg for CBS and ABC News—they were asking passersby for their views on the emergency—were arrested and had their film confiscated. Wim De Vos, a CBS cameraman who had been living in South Africa with his family for eleven years, was summarily expelled from the country four days later, and Richard Manning, chief correspondent for *Newsweek* (and an aggressive questioner at the Bureau for Information briefings), was deported within a fortnight for writing a story about the emergency that contained the observation "P. W. Botha has turned a racist regime into a police state." (The offending *Newsweek* was unavailable in South Africa, the local distributor having been intimidated by the government. That week's issue of *Time* was in the stores—with four blank pages where the dispatch from South Africa belonged.)

Foreign television is especially feared and loathed by the government. To the emergency ban on filming unrest was soon added a ban on live satellite transmissions, which meant that all news footage leaving the country had to do so on videotape, through government facilities. But those correspondents who bothered to show up at the Bureau for Information's briefings discovered how sensitive the authorities could also be to the printed word. Individual reporters were singled out and assailed for individual phrases contained in their dispatches; David Rogers, of Reuters, got his knuckles rapped for calling South Africa a "riot-torn country" and the emergency measures "draconian." Correspondents were warned not to refer to the government as a "white-minority regime"—apparently because there were now two "non-white" (albeit powerless) men in the Cabinet. Louis Nel, the Deputy Minister of Information, let it be known that he would no longer brook use of the word "disappearance" to describe what had befallen the thousands of South Africans who had recently disappeared.

Some overseas newspapers resorted to subterfuge: journalists posed as tourists, stories were filed by telephone and published without bylines. ABC News broadcast a story about how Bishop Tutu was angry with Margaret Thatcher, then had its correspondent in London describe what Tutu was angry about (the British government's opposition to sanctions). On the whole, though, the news organizations followed the new rules, publicly protesting, often running warnings to their readers and viewers that their dispatches had been censored, even holding out the possibility that they might abandon their South African operations, but in the meantime declining to risk their presence in the country for any single story.

In the past, the foreign press had often carried news about South Africa that was unavailable inside South Africa. In 1975, while Percy Qoboza was at Harvard on a Nieman fellowship, he went home for Christmas and discovered that friends there did not even know that South Africa had invaded Angola, although it had been a major world news story for many weeks. A few days before the imposition of the 1986 emergency, television stations in one hundred countries had broadcast scenes of frightening violence at Witwatersrand University as police attacked peaceful demonstrators, but South African viewers saw none of it. The same week, film shown on overseas television had clearly depicted members of the security forces leading vigilantes into battle against comrades in the Crossroads squatter camp outside Cape Town. Again, South Africans were spared these unsettling images (this bit of "black-on-black violence" left fifty-three people dead and seventy thousand homeless).

Under the emergency, however, the outside world would no longer receive larger portions of the truth about what was happening in South Africa than South Africans did. The people of Rome and Chicago would be forced to wear the same Botha-designed blinders that the people of Bloemfontein and Soweto wore. Overseas TV still showed many things that South Africans would never be permitted to see. When SATV aired a BBC debate between the South African ambassador to Britain, a Tory M.P., and ANC President Oliver Tambo, the segment was edited so that South African viewers never even realized that Tambo was there. But those stomach-turning scenes of the police and Army beating and shooting people in the townships, which had done so much to swing the American public in favor of economic sanctions, would not be seen again. "These regulations are very well thought-out," Alan Cowell, of the *New York Times,* told me. "In 1982, John Darnton, the *Times* correspondent in Warsaw, could avoid censorship by sending letters out rather than Telexes. That's impossible here. Even mentioning a detainee's name over the phone is illegal." (In January, 1987, the *Times* bureau in Johannesburg was closed for two months after Cowell antagonized what he called, in a valedictory article, "the high priests of official silence.")

Just about every government in the world, including Pretoria's friends and allies in Bonn, London, and Washington, condemned the state of emergency. In the days following its imposition, the South African ambassador to the United States, Herbert Beukes, spent most of his waking hours on television talk shows defending his government's action. But his story and those of other spokesmen were not always coordinated. While Beukes was telling Americans that the emergency was "a method, a tactic," to control violence by "black faceless people with no political agenda," P. W. Botha was disclosing his laughably specific revolutionary "agenda" and Foreign Minister R. F. Botha was telling South Africans that the emergency was needed "to counter a Marxist revolution." (It may have been, of course, that the Foreign Minister simply did not want his ambassadors overburdening weak-minded foreigners with information. As he told the *Sunday Times* on June 15, "We are dealing with a Western world that is sick.") But sense and consistency have never been the apartheid government's long suit. As Louis Nel explained, after the declaration of the emergency, "There is not press censorship, but there is a limit to what may be published."

As in other areas, the government wanted it both ways. Its leaders extol their defense of "Western Christian values" and "democratic freedoms" while denying those values and freedoms on a vast scale. In the case of the press, the regime both insisted that there was no crisis—Louis Nel attacked one foreign reporter for ignoring "the great deal of normality that most South Africans experience daily," as if grocery shopping were news—and invoked the crisis to justify its extraordinary curbs on the flow of information. "All the agencies of the media must realize that to provide the enemy with intelligence, either knowingly or unknowingly, is treasonable," wrote the chief of the South African military in 1981. And the regime does behave as if it is at war: interning huge numbers of "the enemy," torturing them for information, militarizing every corner of South African life. But woe betide the reporter who describes the situation as a war.

What has never been demonstrated is that the South African security establishment understands its "enemy"—a problem that is especially obvious in its own propaganda. The voluminous disinformation that it directs at blacks, mostly in the form of phony pamphlets, is generally so crude that it sows more hilarity than confusion. The security forces either overestimate the credulity of township residents, expecting them to believe that black political organizations are calling for the most foolish measures, or else their staff writers simply cannot master black political idiom. Even relatively straightforward government productions in this field tend to be fiascos. While I was in South Africa, the government published a booklet, titled *Talking to the A.N.C.*, which sought to demonstrate that the ANC was a communist-dominated terrorist organization. What the booklet actually demonstrated was the regime's own attitude toward information, as it quoted extensively but selectively from banned documents and speeches, thus seeking to *ensure* that statements would be taken out of their original contexts. The booklet backfired badly, for it was an instant smash hit in the townships. Not only did it contain the first legally published photograph of Nelson Mandela to appear in the country in twenty-three years, but the fierce, inflammatory quotations from ANC leaders echoed precisely the popular mood. The regime had published seventy thousand copies of *Talking to the A.N.C.*, but stocks ran out in a matter of days. I wanted one for a souvenir, but I could not get anyone to part with theirs.

The Bureau for Information soon began to produce its own fiascos. First it launched, semi-clandestinely, a number of township "community newspapers," none of which fooled anyone. Eventually, it issued a pop song and videotape, called "Together We Will Build a Brighter Future," imitating shamelessly the then-recent "We Are the World" extravaganza, which had helped raise millions of dollars for refugee relief. "Together We Will Build" cost more than four million rands to produce, an expense which only helped fuel the firestorms of ridicule that fell on the government's head in its wake. The song, with its message of "harmony and peace and plenty," was broadcast constantly on state-controlled radio and television, but its main social consequence seemed to be the ostracism suffered by the musicians, particularly the black musicians, who had been induced to play on it.

With journalists, the bureau showed judgment almost as bizarre when it offered to prove its assertions about the peace and harmony that reigned in the blacked-out townships by taking a group of about twenty reporters on an impromptu "tour." The reporters, who were not told their destination, were flown by helicopter from Pretoria to Soweto, where they landed at a police station and were loaded, along with a number of policemen, into police vans with heavily meshed windows. They were then driven around for fifty minutes, during which they were not allowed to leave the vans, before being flown back to Pretoria by helicopter. The coverage that this "mystery tour" received could not possibly have been what the bureau had in mind. No conclusons were drawn about the state of affairs in Soweto, of course, and the only quote in the *Star*'s story was from a reporter who rumbled, "First time I've attended a press conference in a cage." The bureau's David Steward said more than he knew when he announced the following day, "We are still in the process of perfecting the free flow of information."

Parliamentary privilege still creates, at least in theory, a space in which freedom of speech cannot be abridged in South Africa. Thus, on the day that the state of emergency was declared, Dave Dalling, a Progressive Federal Party M.P. from the wealthy northern suburbs of Johannesburg, thundered, in reference to police torture, that the ruling party's members "would not be able to say 'they did not know,' when the Nuremberg trials are held in South Africa, as they will be." The next day, theory met practice. Dalling, under heavy pressure from the government, retracted his statement, murmuring, "I regret any offence that might have been caused." (The National Party is extraordinarily sensitive about suggestions that its behavior resembles that of the Nazis when they were in power in Germany.)

There was much evidence to suggest that white South Africans on the whole welcomed the new restrictions on the press. As a typical letter to the *Star* from a white reader explained, "I for one (and I am sure the moderate majority of all races hold similar views) am thoroughly sick and tired of the destructive bleatings of the liberal media," and suggested that newspapers "should cease their endless carping criticism, and resolve to enjoy the Press freedom currently available to them under the new State of Emergency measures."

Opinion surveys published just as the emergency got underway offered some strange but irresistible glimpses into white political thinking. One showed that, although most whites believed that "civil war" was unavoidable, they did not believe that blacks had legitimate grievances—indeed, only nineteen percent of National Party supporters agreed that blacks had legitimate grievances. Most attributed the unrest in the townships to foreigners, agitators, "specifically communist agitators," said the university professor who conducted the survey. (The convenient idea that their country is besieged by communists is widespread among white South Africans, but P. W. Botha himself put the best spin on this notion that I've heard when, in 1983, he was speaking to a crowd about his plans for blacks and a heckler yelled, "Give them all the vote." Botha's retort: "No, my friend, I am not a communist.") Another survey, this one conducted by the quasi-governmental Human Sciences Research Council, releasing its findings on the same day, showed that, among whites in small Transvaal towns, "double the number of people would leave their towns if blacks shared the swimming baths as they would if the town became embroiled in a guerrilla war."

The complaints so often heard among black journalists—that the press, including the English-language papers, had done little to alleviate white ignorance or challenge white assumptions or cast light on black reality for white readers—were certainly borne out by such polls. The whites in question, of course, tended to blame the press for telling them *too much* about what was wrong in the country, if not for creating most of the trouble itself. As Jon Qwelane said, "They blame the thermometer for the weather."

Chapter 13

"They Are Playing Marbles with Our Country"

When word reached the *Star* newsroom, on the day after the announcement of the emergency, that that day's editions of the *Sowetan* and the *Weekly Mail* had been banned, the mood in the ghetto was dismal indeed. Qwelane turned off his monitor and sat, shoulders sagging, staring into space. Finally, he said, "I feel defeated. How can you try to write something sensible in a situation of senselessness? *This* is the time to cry for the beloved country. We are ruled by imbeciles. They are playing marbles with our country. I don't want to write anything. I can't find the words."

Qwelane shook his head.

We sat in silence.

A few minutes later, Phil Mtimkulu and Maud Motanyane arrived. They took seats at a desk opposite us, where Mtimkulu began unpacking a large parcel of fish and chips. Qwelane looked up, his eyes full of fire and gloom, but his voice gentle as he asked, "Maud, have you seen the film *The Lion Is Feeding*?"

Motanyane shook her head.

Qwelane nodded at Mtimkulu. "You are about to see it," he said.

Mtimkulu, just on the point of plunging into a greasy pile of food, froze, and rolled his eyes up to look at Qwelane. They stared at each other. Neither of them smiled. Motanyane and I collapsed with laughter. It was a perfect instance of the wry resilience, the lilting, ferocious *esprit de corps* that distinguished black reporters even in this dark time.

Mtimkulu had called a meeting the previous afternoon to discuss how they would cover events on June 16. The plan was to have people in each of the major townships at least a day in advance, in case the security forces sealed some areas completely; to work on foot, probably incognito; to phone in every hour, if possible; and to return to town the following day. Even if the paper could not publish the stories they collected, the reporters would at least have some idea of what was happening. So they were making arrangements for places to stay. Mudini Maivha would be going into Alexandra over the weekend—the 16th was a Monday—and staying at the home of a friend. Mtimkulu himself would be covering the Vaal Triangle. Maud Motanyane would be in KwaThema. Mike Tissong would be in Eldorado Park. Montshiwa Moroke and Mike Siluma would be in Soweto.

The *Star* management had surprised its township reporters by issuing each of them a safe-conduct. Dated June 16, 1986, and addressed "To Whom It May Concern," the letter, written on *Star* letterhead stationery and signed by the paper's general manager, confirmed that its bearer was a *Star* employee and asked that he or she be allowed to proceed unhindered. It quoted from a joint statement issued on June 2 by three leading resistance organizations—the UDF, the Congress of South African Trade Unions, and the National Education Crisis Committee—as follows: "All freedom-loving South Africans will abstain from any form of work to participate in June 16 activities in all areas. This will, of course, exclude nurses, doctors and journalists." I found this letter extraordinary: an acknowledgement by the *Star* management that the resistance constituted an authority in some ways more powerful than the state. But the *Star*'s black reporters did not share my amazement. They read the letters, laughed humorlessly, and threw them in the wastebasket.

Qwelane was not sure what he would be doing on June 16. He

had been invited to Paris to speak to a United Nations conference on that day. The conference organizers had sent him an air ticket. His superiors at the *Star* had ordered him not to go, but their admonitions did not seem to weigh heavily in his deliberations. "This would be the first June 16 I haven't covered since 1976," he told me. "My heart tells me I should stay, but my head tells me I should go." The conference was the World Conference for Economic Sanctions Against South Africa. Wouldn't he be likely to have trouble when he came home? Qwelane shrugged. "I don't say anything outside that I won't say inside. But I don't really care if there is some reprisal for something I've said outside. It's no skin off my nose. It's not my passport. It's theirs. They can take it away."

In the meantime, Qwelane was working hard—fighting off the listlessness that threatened to engulf him and the other reporters under the new restrictions. He had written a long feature about 1976 and two strong columns—one an open letter to P. W. Botha denouncing the emergency, the other recounting a conversation with a friend in which each sought to find out the other's plans for the June 16 work stoppage without uttering a subversive statement. (" 'Will you be travelling by taxi to work tomorrow morning?' 'No, and you?' I retorted. 'No,' he said. 'Well, what are you going to use? A bus or a train?' I asked. 'Nothing of the sort,' he replied. 'But you surely won't walk the distance, will you?' I ventured. 'No,' he said, with a ring of defiance in his voice. The picture was becoming clearer.") Qwelane and Alf Kumalo had come up with a story for the *Sunday Star,* which they enjoined me to keep to myself, so that the people on the daily wouldn't grab it. It was an interview with the sister of Hector Petersen, the thirteen-year-old martyr of the 1976 uprising. Kumalo had already been to the place where she worked. "Her employer's friendly," he reported. "He gives you coffee, and he says she can say *anything she likes.*" Though Kumalo and Qwelane were excited about it, it was unlikely that this piece would be enough to mollify the *Star*'s editors if Qwelane defied them and left for Paris. In the end, on June 15, he did fly to Paris, and the editors were, from all accounts, furious.

*   *   *

But Qwelane did not miss much on June 16. After he had refused to write "BLACK LEADERS APPEAL FOR CALM," the editors acknowledged the problem in the *Sunday Star*'s lead editorial, writing, "We earnestly appeal for calm, even though the emergency seems to mock the appeal." The anniversary stay-away, despite the government's attempts to undermine it, was a major success: two million black workers boycotted their jobs, leaving the cities deserted and the economy paralyzed. But no great confrontation occurred—at least, none that anyone seemed to know about.

It was very hard to get information. Journalists were banned from the townships. (The *Star* reporters were already inside the townships, but they were unable to move around freely, because of the heavy police presence, and they gathered little news.) Telephone service from all the major townships suddenly and inexplicably went dead on the 16th. The only phones working, it seemed, were those in the township police stations. (At a Bureau for Information briefing, the government's explanation that this magnificent coincidence was due to "technical problems" met with stunned silence. When the government spokesman added that similar power problems had occurred in New York City, an American reporter observed that the New York power failures were actually different in that they had affected both black and white homes.) The security forces, bolstered by a massive call-up of soldiers, patrolled the empty township streets in their V-bottomed armored personnel carriers. Pamphlets warning people to stay indoors were dropped from airplanes; loudspeakers mounted on the airplanes boomed the same warning down at residents—all this on what the government was insisting was "a normal working day." (The Bureau for Information claimed that the story about the pamphlets was "devoid of all truth" and warned papers not to publish it. The *Star* informed the bureau that it had proof. Finally, on June 19, David Steward reversed himself and admitted that it was true.)

There were violent incidents—the Bureau for Information reported the next day that eleven people had been killed, four by security forces in the eastern Cape, the others in "black-on-black violence"—but the general situation seemed to be as the *Star* editors had hoped: "calm." The "evil plan" that the government claimed to have uncovered for resistance on June 16—the ten thousand arsonists marching from KwaThema on the Union Buildings, for instance—had been rank fantasy. But whatever activities the resistance *had* planned—beyond the stayaway—were, it was clear, decisively cancelled by the repression.

I got up early on the 16th and tried to find some news on the radio. Finally, at 7:45 A.M., I heard, "And a special report this morning," and turned up the volume. The announcer continued, "We'll be investigating the controversy surrounding weight loss in jockeys." I ended up going to a service at St. Mary's Cathedral, in downtown Johannesburg, Bishop Tutu conducting. The streets outside were as silent as on a Sunday, except for small groups of police in field dress who patrolled the sidewalks, and trucks full of sullen young soldiers that occasionally rumbled past. (Johannesburg, which looks much like Akron, Ohio, is hard to accept as the setting for the world's most interesting revolution at the best of times. With its streets devoid of Africans—who call the place Egoli, the city of gold, which at least evokes the great warren of tunnels beneath one's feet, and the millions of miners whose dark, dangerous, mind-wrenchingly meaningless work created the wealth that built and sustains the city—its dullness is actually frightening.)

About five hundred people were at the service, the great majority of them white. Famous faces dotted the crowd—Beyers Naude, the dissident Afrikaner clergyman; Tony Bloom, the liberal tycoon; Allister Sparks—and what appeared to be the whole foreign press corps jammed the cathedral's nave, with klieg lights, cameras, and cannon mikes wrapped in blankets. A large floral garland leaned against the foot of the pulpit: a symbol of white good will that Tutu would be taking to Soweto. A similar garland had been confiscated from him that morning at a roadblock, Tutu said, "where those flowers are now being trampled underfoot by the security forces." He had been stopped at roadblocks and searched twice that morning, despite his cassock and his fame, "and that is good: to be reminded that what matters in South Africa is that you are black." Tutu's sermon, condemning the state of emergency, the mass detentions, the ban on June 16 services, and all violence, was eloquent and undoubtedly illegal. At one point, he asked his listeners, "Do you believe we have a great country?" The answering "Yes" was uncertain. He repeated the question. A louder "Yes" resounded through the cathedral. Tutu: "Do you believe we have some really wonderful people, black and white, here?" "YES!" roared the crowd. Tutu: "Then why are we allowing our country to be destroyed?"

The audience was silent.

After Tutu had finished, the crowd broke into "Nkosi Sikelel iAfrika," led by a black woman with a magnificent, soaring voice. All the blacks in the church raised their fists as they sang. A few whites raised their fists, too.

The raised fist was outlawed by an emergency regulation promulgated a few days later. So were outdoor funerals, T-shirts bearing the names or symbols of any of 47 organizations, and the publication of any statement by any officer of any of 118 organizations in the western Cape.

In the white areas, June 16 was exceedingly quiet. *City Press* ran a tongue-in-cheek front-page story under the head "WHITE PUPILS' FIRST STAYAWAY." About one-third of the country's white schoolchildren, it seemed, had been kept home by worried parents on the big day. The photograph that ran with the *City Press* story showed an older white man in a green track suit standing at a classroom window, talking into an orange two-way radio, and looking out worriedly while, in the background, a scattering of children in school uniforms worked at their desks. The caption read, "It's June 16—and white people are on the alert. One of them, Bill Bronkhorst, patrols a classroom in Johannesburg's General De la Rey School—just one of the parents, mostly armed, who joined in stringent security measures at white schools in the Transvaal on Monday."

Things were also tense, for somewhat better reason, in the house where I was staying. Nobody in the house—a rambling place with a fluctuating population that numbered, when I arrived, seven or eight—was detained or thought to be a police target, but several of us knew people (activists, lawyers, union officials) who were on the run, and the house was an occasional refuge for some of them. One person, the wife of a well-known trade unionist and community leader whom the authorities have harassed mercilessly for years, came to stay with us. She was quiet and sad, passing hours knitting by the fireplace alone. Once or twice, late in the evening, she talked to me about how much she missed her children and her husband, and her voice filled with fury when she said, "How dare these people, how *dare* they." We called her by a pseudonym, even around the supper table, to try to prevent the children in the house from repeating her name inadvertently somewhere.

Discretion was also exercised around a young accountancy student who lived in the house. Her name was Emerald. She was twenty years old, short, white, dark-haired, with a high, friendly voice and a blunt, cockney manner. Emerald's father was dead, her mother was an alcoholic, and she had come to live with the family who owned the rambling house when she was seventeen. After a miserable, impoverished childhood in a cramped apartment in Hillbrow, she had two rooms of her own, tolerant, sober people around her, and no one but herself to take care of. One of her rooms, her "study," she had painted bright blue and yellow and furnished with two black swivel chairs, a huge blue fluffy carnival-prize dog, and a lamp with a yellow bulb. Emerald went to a whites-only technical college where the other students, she said, were shamelessly racist. She knew better than to be that way herself—thanks, it seemed, to her long, gentle exposure to liberal ideas in her adopted family.

Emerald had a boyfriend, though, an ex-Rhodesian of Greek extraction named Greg. Greg gave the distinct impression that he had never been exposed to the sort of ideas that distinguished Emerald from her classmates—or, if he had, that they had not seduced him. I never heard Greg talk politics. He worked as an automobile mechanic and seemed quite uneasy with the sort of university-educated liberals and leftists who tended to congregate at the house, and he rarely opened his mouth. But the fact that he did not spoke volumes under the circumstances. Greg had friends, it was said, who were policemen. After the state of emergency was imposed, Greg made everyone in the house nervous, and there was talk of asking Emerald not to bring him around for a while. Nobody seemed to know how to broach the subject, though, since we weren't sure if Emerald had noticed that there *was* a state of emergency, or if she believed the stories the children were told about why all these people had started showing up at odd hours. In the end, nothing was said, at least not while I was around.

I considered moving to less tense quarters myself. If the house was raided, I was sure that I would be arrested and deported. My room was full of evidence—books, notebooks, newspaper clippings—that I was not the innocent surfer I had impersonated on my visa application. I was taking precautions: photocopying my notes every few days, making two copies and caching one while sending the other back to the United States. But I wasn't sleeping well, fretting that every vehicle I heard stopping on the street outside at night would be the police. Then a friend—a foreign journalist, who was staying in an international hotel in downtown Johannesburg—told me that she thought it was actually worse where she was. She felt watched all the time, did not trust the hotel post office, and had been refused the use of the hotel's Telex machine when its operator noticed that the first paragraph of her dispatch to her paper contained the word "emergency." I stayed in the house—and away from Greg.

I had taken to writing up my notes in the reading room of the public library, which was near the *Star* offices. The librarian there was a soft-spoken, very handsome, middle-aged black man named Sam. He would watch me come in and work, the lone *umlungu* among the hundreds of black high school students who hid there in the peaceful, book-lined silence with their textbooks for Ecological Biology I, their study-aid notes for *The Great Gatsby*. Usually, before I left, I would pay Sam to photocopy my notes. One afternoon, I was too late to get to the post office, so I asked him to hold the copies for me. If I didn't return for them,

I said, I would send for them. Sam regarded me thoughtfully for a moment, then stacked the copies on a shelf without a word. A few days later, he asked me, "For how long are you doing this project?"

A month or two, I told him.

"Well, then," he said, "you really should know that this is not the story here. Things are really not like this." He indicated the dreary, bustling city outside. "For instance, this morning, at the train station in Soweto, I saw a big pool of blood. There were people killed there last night, apparently. There was a lot of blood."

Sam peered into my eyes to see if I understood—understood what it was that all the students in the reading room were hiding *from*. He knew I was American, knew I was a writer, that was all. A great many people, I thought—even some who were convinced of the world's indifference to their plight—really wanted their story told outside.

Chapter 14

Kidnappings, Bombs, and Dog Shows

By the second week of the emergency, it was widely known that a number of journalists were in police custody, including Andre Koopman, of the *Cape Times,* arrested with an entire church congregation in Cape Town; Mike Loewe, of the *Weekly Mail*; Theophilus Mashiane, a television sound man; Brian Sokutu, a freelancer from Port Elizabeth; and Mathata Tsedu, of the *Sowetan.* Progressive Federal Party M.P.s, utilizing parliamentary privilege, had read out a list of people believed to be detained, including these, during debates in the House of Assembly. But then, on June 25, Parliament adjourned, shutting down the one forum in which those who had been jailed or had vanished might be named.

The next night, Zwelakhe Sisulu, the editor of *New Nation,* was at home in Dube, Soweto, when four white men, two of them wearing balaclavas, broke down his front gate and, without identifying themselves, abducted him at gunpoint in an unmarked jeep. Sisulu is probably the best-known black journalist in South Africa. He is the son of Walter Sisulu, a top ANC leader, who has been serving a life sentence for sabotage since 1964. Zwelakhe's mother, Albertina, who has been banned almost continuously for over twenty years, is also a major resistance figure. Zwelakhe, who began his career as a reporter at the *Rand Daily Mail,* has been detained many times, was banned in 1980 for three years, together with Phil Mtimkulu and other MWASA officers, and spent eight months in solitary confinement in 1982. A Nieman fellow in 1984, Sisulu returned to South Africa to found *New Nation* in 1985. *New Nation* was an obvious target for suppression under the emergency. I was in the paper's offices on the day before Sisulu's disappearance, and I thought that the mood there bordered on the hysterical. "You can run, but you can't hide!" one young photographer kept shouting, provoking choruses of wild laughter from his office mates. Sisulu himself was calm. He told me that the paper was operating normally, that he and his colleagues had decided that the state was planning not to detain them but simply to harass them and see if it could stop production of the paper by driving the editors underground.

Word of Sisulu's disappearance reached the *Star* newsroom the following day, and was filed along with all the other detentions that could not be reported. But Qwelane, who had returned from Paris a few days before, decided to follow it up. He phoned Zodwa, Sisulu's wife, and Albertina for details, and when he put down the phone he said, in a shocked voice, "This is no ordinary detention. They never identified themselves as cops. So he is completely at their mercy. I'm going to write it up as a crime story, a kidnapping." Qwelane turned to a terminal and started writing.

When he was finished, he immediately began lobbying the *Star*'s editors to get the piece in the next day's paper. Qwelane's object, unstated but understood, was to force the hand of the police—to raise the alarm and compel the authorities to admit that they had Sisulu, if they in fact had him. Although plenty of "politicals" had died in custody, Sisulu was definitely safer if the world knew that the police had him than if the police were in a position to deny all knowledge of him. On the other hand, if the police denied having detained him, they would at least have to open an investigation of his kidnapping.

Qwelane's story ran on the front page the next day. Minister of

Law and Order Louis Le Grange was reportedly livid. Even before the *Star* hit the stands, he had been deluged by queries from opposition M.P.s and overseas groups about Sisulu's status. Apparently hoping to avert publication of the kidnapping story, he had let it be known privately that his men did have the editor in custody. But the *Star* piece, as Qwelane had hoped, forced his hand, and Sisulu soon became the first—and, for a long while, the only—person whom Pretoria officially admitted having detained under the state of emergency.

I watched this drama from close range, and was delighted by its outcome. More so, it seemed, than Qwelane was. He accepted with good grace the compliments of his colleagues on his ploy and its result, but he did not linger over the episode, except to worry that Le Grange might decide to take some revenge on him personally. There wasn't much to relish or celebrate, of course. Sisulu was still in jail, along with thousands of other people. There was, perhaps, the satisfaction of having let the security forces know they were being watched—the revelation that the police were going about their business in unmarked vehicles and wearing balaclavas was surely rather embarrassing—and of having given the public a glimpse of what the state was doing. But the mood among the black reporters on the *Star* seemed to preclude professional satisfaction. "Really, you just lose your enthusiasm to report about things," Phil Mtimkulu told me. "The ban on meetings and unrest coverage means we are virtually unemployed. You just don't feel like covering dog shows."

Rex Gibson had instructed *Star* reporters to report normally, insofar as that was possible, simply filing their stories and letting the editors and lawyers worry about what could be printed. A dossier was being kept of important stories that were not being run. Yet morale is everything among the black reporters, and timing is everything in news, and following up tips required a blind faith that was impossible to muster. There was a strong, sustained bus boycott going on in Duduza. A woman had been killed in Soweto by plainclothes policemen. Calls were constantly coming in from little, far-flung townships reporting abuses and deaths never mentioned by the Bureau for Information. These were all stories that would normally have drawn energetic coverage. As it was, they received none, for they could not be published, and no one believed that the emergency would end soon. One afternoon in the ghetto, Mtimkulu scanned the *Star*'s front page, with its array of Xs indicating censored stories, and said, to no one in particular, "You know, this paper looks better with restrictions than without them."

One resistance leader I talked with, a high UDF official, took Phil's idea a step further. He suggested that the Argus papers—he didn't say whether he meant the editors or the owners or both—secretly welcomed the state of emergency and the new press restrictions, because of their concern that full coverage of the uprising would discourage foreign investment. We were sitting on a bench in a park on the outskirts of Johannesburg at the time. It was a cold, beautiful afternoon; acres of empty, winter-brown highveld stretched around us. My companion was in hiding, so our rendezvous had been a complex series of maneuvers, involving several car transfers and some impressive timing, that culminated in the quiet, intense conversation on the bench—from which we could survey about a mile of the only road that entered the park. We fell silent when a car appeared, and resumed talking only when we saw that the car contained only a woman and two small children. We fell silent again when a young black man came walking across the veld in our direction. He carried a big silver radio on one shoulder, from which *mbaqanga* music spilled, and he crossed into a grove of eucalyptus just down the slope from where we sat. As he passed, the young man turned and smiled knowingly at us. I wondered if he was connected in some way to my companion—a well-camouflaged sentry, perhaps. My companion made no sign. He resumed talking about the way big capital, through the English press, was trying to promote forms of black nationalism that it believed it could control.

One afternoon, about three weeks into the emergency, Qwelane was on the telephone trying to reach the ANC in Lusaka. The Bureau for Information had been trumpeting the charges of a Lusaka lawyer, recently arrived in South Africa, that the Zambian government had been persecuting him, the inescapable subtext being that black governments trample on human rights more thoroughly than a certain white government does, so that their victims are compelled to flee to the land of milk, honey, and civilized behavior: South Africa. The ANC stood accused of being an accomplice in his torment. What Qwelane, along with other experienced Pretoria watchers, suspected was that the lawyer was a South African spy who had been unmasked. What Qwelane wanted was an interview, and then to bounce the lawyer's remarks about the Zambian government and the ANC off the Zambians and the ANC. But the bureau was keeping its man under wraps, exposing him only to friendly reporters and the television news, where his story was playing in nightly installments. Qwelane therefore had to work in reverse: get some provocative comments about the case from Zambia if he could, then go to the bureau with the argument that its star performer should have a chance to answer these serious charges. Qwelane was having trouble raising anyone in Lusaka, though, and he held the phone away from his good ear so that he could also hear the conversations going on around him in the ghetto.

People were telling stories about police attacks on funerals. The young white reporter with the rooster-tail haircut was listening intently. She had changed since the beginning of the emergency. Maud Motanyane said that it was her indignation over seeing the *Star*'s list of people believed to be detained, which she had kept and updated assiduously, suppressed. "It has politicized her," Motanyane said, with some wonderment. "She can't believe they won't print her list." Now she listened to the tales of tear gas and unprovoked shootings with her face twisted in concern. "I just don't understand *why* the Army would attack," she said. No one could enlighten her. (I had once said roughly the same thing to Bishop Tutu, and he had said angrily, "They want to kill. They don't know how to deal with peace. And a lot of them want to shoot and kill.")

But covering funerals already seemed a thing of the past. Herbert Mabuza said glumly, "Now we just sit and wait for a bomb to go off." There had been a rash of bombings since the imposition of the emergency, including several in downtown Johannesburg. The police, who attributed every blast to the ANC, were generally delighted to have these "terrorist" acts publicized, although they often restricted photographs of the damage, not wanting to alarm the public unduly. After one blast, Leon Mellett of the Bureau for Information told the *Star* that it could publish its photos only if they showed the ANC in a "cruel light"; if they showed the ANC in a favorable light, the paper would be prosecuted.

A few days before, I had arrived at the *Star* newsroom and had been surprised to find the place deserted; it was just before the day's last deadline, normally a frantic hour. I found a secretary at the news desk, a middle-aged white woman, who looked at me in horror when I asked if my interview with one of the editors was still on. She exclaimed, "Not now! Not today! Don't you know what's happened? They've just blown up the Wimpy Bar in Rissik Street!" The woman was literally wringing her hands in anguish. I made my apologies and wandered down to the ghetto, where I found Maud Motanyane working quietly at a terminal. I asked why she was not out at the bomb site, which was only a few blocks away. Maud gave me a look of monumental boredom— and I thought the contrast between her attitude and that of the news-desk secretary said it all about the split news values that prevail under apartheid. No one had been killed in the hamburger-stand blast, but the late final was being held for the story, and all the white papers would play it as a major, if not a historic, event because it actually injured several white shoppers. A few minutes later, a stampede of reporters and photographers—including Herbert Mabuza, who had beaten the police to the site and gotten good color pictures—thundered into the newsroom, sprinting to their terminals and darkrooms to try to get their copy into the late final.

It was almost possible to forget all the onerous curbs on reporting that had obtained *before* the emergency. A few evenings earlier, I had received a sharp reminder of some of those when I asked Jo-Anne Collinge, the one white reporter on the *Star*'s

Africa edition, about the worst case of torture she had seen. Collinge thought for a moment, then described a fourteen-year-old boy who had been picked up by the Army, blindfolded, dunked in dirty water, had bare electrical cables wound around his fingers, been shocked repeatedly, burned with a cigarette lighter, and set alight. He had been held for a week. Collinge, who has a spunky, quick-to-laugh manner, sighed heavily. "But like so many of these cases, it was a problem to publish," she said. "The police will inevitably subpoena the reporter and demand to know your sources. If you give them any names, there will be reprisals. If you identify the victim, they will go and find him and finish him off. In this case, the boy was blindfolded, so he could not tell us exactly where the Army camp was. It was only a temporary camp, anyway. In the end, I didn't write the story. It saw the light of day eventually, though, in a report by a group of American human-rights lawyers."

While we talked, Collinge, who was on night duty, periodically called up the wire services on her terminal to check the latest stories. At one point, she suddenly exclaimed, "A witch burning! I don't believe it. The news desk missed a witch burning. This must have been on there all day." She explained: "The editors love witch burnings. They always send somebody out to these villages to photograph the gory remains and talk to the neighbors. I never go, because there's usually no one out there who speaks English—the places where these things happen are really remote. The black reporters have to go, but they hate it. The editors seem to think that our white readers just love these stories of, you know, 'African barbarism,' and I suppose they're right. Sometimes they throw in a progressive anthropologist to explain why these things happen. But what a stroke of luck that they missed this!"

I wondered about other chestnuts at the *Star*.

Collinge rattled off a few: "Mixed couples. White priest who lives in a black township. White political trials. Black waifs on the streets in Hillbrow—which we call 'The Twilight Children,' because that's usually its title. And, of course, there's always 'New Hope in South West,' which runs every second month, alternating, as it has done for the past fifteen years, with 'Hope Fades in South West.' "

Qwelane gave up on Lusaka for the day, put down the phone, and turned to a terminal. The previous day's *Sunday Star* lay on a desk. It was the one with the banner front-page headline "FREE MANDELA NOW," and it occurred to me that this story, too, was a *Star* chestnut: white businessmen endorsing some reform. Every well-known capitalist in South Africa seemed to have contributed a statement to the piece—even Sol Kerzner, a tycoon resort developer who is a sort of South African Donald Trump. Somehow, the story was hard to take seriously; certainly none of the black reporters seemed to do so. That day's *City Press* carried a column that had become a regular feature: "How to Trace a Detainee." The column included information on what hours "toiletries and clothing" could be left at police headquarters in John Vorster Square—"on Fridays, between 8 A.M. and 10 A.M." This was the sort of story that blacks *could* be expected to take seriously these days, and it measured, once more, the distance between a paper like the *Star,* which would never carry anything like it, and black life. *City Press,* moreover, was a mainstream paper, owned by Nasionale Pers. Community papers, "alternative" papers, were themselves under full-scale assault. Just a few blocks from the *Star*, the offices of *SASPU National,* a left-wing student newspaper at Witwatersrand University, had been raided by the police and then, a few days later, to absolutely no one's surprise, destroyed by fire.

I watched Qwelane work, pecking quickly at the keyboard with one finger of his left hand, two of his right. He was working that afternoon on a story about the repeal of the pass laws—the laws that had long controlled the lives of blacks at the most basic level, restricting their movements inside South Africa. The repeal had become official a few days before. The event had been a grand anticlimax. Although the government had sought to portray the repeal, both internationally and domestically, as a fundamental reform of apartheid, and although the pass laws had in fact been both a cornerstone of the apartheid system and the target of countless black protests over the years, the reaction in the townships to their repeal had been nonexistent. Two years before, perhaps, black people would have celebrated such a move on the part of the government, but events had outpaced this sort of piecemeal "reform." Nothing short of majority rule—that is, the complete abolition of apartheid—was likely to satisfy many blacks now. Besides, there were indications that more stringent laws against trespassing, vagrancy, and squatting would effectively replace the unwieldy pass laws as the official control on black urbanization. Blacks still needed "approved housing" in order to live in the cities, and millions of residents of the so-called "independent" bantustans still needed work permits, because they were now considered foreigners.

Just how ineffectual the pass laws had become was evident, in fact, from Qwelane's answer to my question about his own "*dompas*." He said, "I lost it in about '75 or '76, when I was mugged on the train from Mafeking. I applied for a new one, but they told me I must go to the Transkeian Embassy. They like to list my birthplace as 'Bophuthatswana,' but they tell me I'm a citizen of the Transkei, because my father was Xhosa." Transkei is the bantustan for Xhosa-speaking people; Mafeking, Qwelane's birthplace, is in what is now Bophuthatswana, the bantustan for Tswana speakers. "I refused to go to their so-called embassy—in fact, they closed the place in 1980, after some kind of mickey-mouse diplomatic row. They later opened another one in the Carlton Centre"—a shopping center in downtown Johannesburg—"but it was bombed, and now, as far as I know, there isn't one. In any case, I've just lived without a pass since that time. I've been picked up, but I've managed to talk my way out of going to jail by using my press pass."

The editors of the *Star,* to the disappointment and disgust of their black reporters, had written that the repeal of the pass laws "should be welcomed with enthusiasm and applause." Qwelane had gone out to assess black reaction—and to expose as a fraud the new "nonracial" identification cards being issued to blacks. The government claimed that forty-five thousand blacks had already applied for the new cards. Qwelane doubted the government's figures. I had gone with him to the Johannesburg pass

office, where the applications were being taken, and we had
found only a handful of people. "Even these people are here only
because they heard on TV that thousands were applying," Qwelane said. We went to several government offices in the West
Rand and never found a crowd. I posed as a white South African
at one place, and Qwelane's suspicions about a racial aspect to the
new cards were confirmed when I was asked only for a birth
certificate; blacks were being required to produce a variety of
documents.

Qwelane attacked the story with gusto, digging through the
Star's files to find stories about the first person issued an old-style
pass—this for purposes of historical analogy—and telling me,
"I'm going to use every trick in the book to make this story
readable. I'm going to write it in the 'Once upon a time' line.
'Once upon a time, there was a man named Jack, who lived in a
suburb of Pretoria named Mamelodi. In 1954, he applied for a
pass. But he didn't live happily ever after.' " Personally, I was
pleased to be making it into the story as a character—as "a white
reporter"—but I doubted that it would be one of Qwelane's
finest. He seemed to feel the same way as he banged out a
conclusion, studied it unhappily awhile, and dispatched it to his
editor.

He opened a can of Coca-Cola. Alf Kumalo said, "You must
stop drinking all that Coke."

Qwelane chuckled and patted his waistline. "I am developing
a tummy," he admitted.

"Sooner or later, you will become shapeless, which is not nice
for a young man, especially one who has had a good figure,"
Kumalo said.

Now people in the ghetto were reminiscing: about dead or
exiled colleagues; about working at newspapers since banned or
bankrupted; about the Star's miserable performance during a
1983 whites-only referendum that approved a new racist constitution, when the paper's editors waffled so long on the issue that
someone ultimately posted a notice in the newsroom: "The Editor's Indecision Is Final." (This was before Rex Gibson came to
the Star; Gibson's predecessor was—and his successor is—Har-

vey Tyson.) Conversation turned to the many deficiencies of the *Star*'s cars and Qwelane recalled that, when Harry Mashabela had been compelled to travel by motorbike, one of his tricks was to leave the motorbike in a distant township, take buses and taxis back to the office, and then tell the racist transport manager that the bike just would not run, leaving him with the headache of retrieving it. Everyone in the ghetto laughed at that.

Phil Mtimkulu caught my eye and pointed with a glance across the low partition into the sports department. In the far corner, a young white reporter in a military uniform—a reservist who had been mobilized—was typing at a terminal. Short blond hair, shiny black boots, and a beret tucked smartly into a loop on the shoulder of his fatigues made the man look for all the world as if he had just jumped out of a Hippo. His presence, as such, was distinctly alarming. And, if I found the soldier a jarring sight in the newsroom, I hated to think how the black reporters found him. Mtimkulu murmured to me, "You see?" and I did not ask what he meant. But I did wonder what the soldier thought of those billboard-sized photos on the newsroom walls, of the burning oil-storage tank and the triumphant guerrilla. Perhaps he had worked at the *Star* for years—normally not in uniform, surely— and he no longer saw them. (After six weeks, I scarcely saw them myself.) But what did he think of his black colleagues? Had he ever spoken to one of them?

I got up and took a walk around the newsroom. Near the elevators, I stopped and read a notice posted in a glass-fronted box. It was a Xeroxed "Code of Ethics," introduced by a note from Harvey Tyson, which read, in part, "Despite curbs on Press freedom, The Star is still a good newspaper. Its balance and its fairness and its philosophy do not allow it to be the world's most famous campaigner for any ideological cause, but its standards are such that The Star has been described by many top international newspapermen, both liberal and conservative, as 'the best newspaper in Africa'—even 'one of the best in the world.' " The appended Code of Ethics, the editor wrote, "will be used to check our performance in the years ahead, under any form of Rightwing or Leftwing government." The code itself was full of unexceptionable ideals. It was only the *Star*'s actual situation in South Africa that made many of them read strangely.

> The Star has a responsibility to be independent of both government and commerce [the code said]. It has a responsibility in overall terms to be constructive, but not misleadingly optimistic or bland. . . . It also has a responsibility to all people in this country to reflect the problems, needs and frustrations of those who have no real political rights and no real political voice. . . . The Star reports news without regard to its own interests or viewpoint and without favour to its advertisers. . . . The Star and its staff must be free of obligations to news sources and special interests. . . . It must give all sides of an issue, with balanced presentation, lack of bias, and no distortion through undue emphasis or omission.

People were collecting themselves to go home. Montshiwa Moroke, who had been on the telephone all afternoon saying "Ah-ha!" and writing furiously, hung up, paged through his notes, and shook his head. "I can't use *any* of this," he said. Then he turned to Mtimkulu and Mabuza, who had been reliving the good old days at the *Rand Daily Mail,* and reminded them, "You always had to have a rugby angle at the *Mail,* too." Moroke was referring to the permanent difficulty of getting "black" stories into white papers—the idea being that, if you could somehow work a little rugby, which is a white South African obsession, into your story, its chances of seeing print improved enormously. Mtimkulu and Mabuza did not disagree.

Qwelane was back at a terminal, having retrieved his piece about the new IDs. As each of the other reporters left, he called out "*Ciao!*" When Maud Motanyane picked up her purse, he said, "Good night, my dear." She replied, "Good night, my dear." But Qwelane kept staring at the video screen, smoking cigarettes and looking dissatisfied. Finally he said, "They've got us doing nothing but reacting to them. They change a law, they issue a new ID, they produce some clown who says the ANC is evil and the Boers are humane, then we run around trying to discredit them. We cannot initiate anything, or investigate anything, in this atmosphere."

Mudini Maivha, who was working on a terminal nearby, said something in what sounded like Shangaan.

I asked for a translation.

Maivha said, "It's a saying. It means, 'The dog with a bone in his mouth cannot bark.' "

Qwelane stubbed out a cigarette and said, "Well, that's it. I am not going to sit around here waiting for a bomb to go off. What is that priest's name in KwaNdebele, the one who can get us Skosana's son?"

"Campbell," I said. I tried not to show my excitement. I had helped put together the leads on the KwaNdebele story, but the *Star*'s editors had pronounced the idea too dangerous and squelched it. I wanted to go, but I had little to lose.

"Let's do it tomorrow," Qwelane said firmly. "If we leave early, while the editors are still in conference, they won't know we're gone until it's too late to stop us. Let's find out what's going on out there."

With that, Qwelane picked up a phone and went back to work.

Chapter 15

Back to
KwaNdebele

Shortly after our trip to see Father Campbell in KwaNdebele, I left South Africa. Qwelane made another trip to KwaNdebele, then wrote a story for the *Sunday Star* that skated close to, if not over, the edge of the emergency regulations. Without revealing that he had gone to KwaNdebele (to do so was, after all, illegal), Qwelane sketched the background to the fighting, recounted in detail the disappearance of the boy who was last seen being loaded into an ambulance, and concluded, without mentioning Father Campbell by name, "Figures and details compiled by sources are a glaring contradiction of the news items published by the Bureau for Information."

The fighting continued in KwaNdebele—over the next few weeks, at least forty members of the Mbokodo vigilantes were reported killed—culminating in a car bomb that "eliminated" Piet Ntuli, the Cabinet strongman, on July 29. Speculation about the identity of Ntuli's assassins ranged from the ANC to the South African police. Conditions in KwaNdebele had become so chaotic, in any case, that even conservative white farmers on the bantustan's borders began making representations to Pretoria to shelve the plans for "independence." In early August, the Kwa-Ndebele government reversed itself and rejected independence.

A spokesman, with breathtaking logic, said, "It is only in a democratic society that a government can heed the wishes of its people. What happened here proves that KwaNdebele is such a society." The Botha government quietly postponed independence.

But then the momentum in KwaNdebele began to shift. In November, Chief Minister Simon Skosana died of natural causes. He was replaced by his former Minister of Home Affairs, George Mahlangu (no relation to Prince James Mahlangu, the leader of the anti-independence forces), and Mbokodo, which had been outlawed and disbanded within hours of Piet Ntuli's death, began to regain strength. Vigilante and police raids on government opponents resumed. Prince James Mahlangu was jailed without charges, along with young Peter Skosana and hundreds of other comrades. On May 5, 1987, the KwaNdebele government, having jailed every visible local opponent of independence, reversed itself again, and called for independence.

The following week, Qwelane, Herbert Mabuza, and Sam Mathe, a driver, went back to KwaNdebele. This time, they were not as lucky as we had been. They were stopped near the shack city of Kwaggafontein, arrested, and locked up with thirty-three other men in a cell built for twelve. Their fellow prisoners included a magistrate, a respected local chief, and the chairman of the KwaNdebele Public Service Commission, all of whom were being detained without charges. Qwelane and his colleagues again took notes on cigarette boxes and scrap paper. They were not allowed to use a telephone, and no one was notified of their arrest. The *Star* editors discovered their whereabouts only by accident on the third day of their incarceration. (A news editor, speaking to the superintendent of a hospital in the area about an unrelated matter, happened to mention that three of his men had gone missing in KwaNdebele. The superintendent, who was also the district surgeon, happened to be making his monthly tour of the bantustan jails the following day. When he discovered that some of the new prisoners in Kwaggafontein were journalists, he recalled his conversation with the editor and alerted the *Star*.) A protest was lodged, and the next day the three men were released.

Qwelane, Mabuza, and Mathe described their experiences in jail in KwaNdebele to the *Star*'s lawyers in sworn affidavits. South Africa's Prisons Act and its Police Act effectively forbid press reports on conditions inside the country's police stations and jails, but the *Star*'s lawyers calculated that signed statements made before a Commissioner of Oaths would stand less chance of provoking charges than a regular, bylined story would. They also hoped that by treating the matter as a crime story the *Star* might avoid, at least in theory—the same theory that had allowed the paper to run Qwelane's story about the "kidnapping" of Zwelakhe Sisulu—violating the emergency regulations that outlawed reporting the actions of the security forces in combatting unrest. So the affidavits formed the bulk of a story that appeared on the front page of the *Sunday Star* on May 24th. The story read, in part:

THREE DAYS IN A HELLHOLE

A magistrate, a senior civil servant, and three *Sunday Star* men were crowded into a cell at a police station where most of thirty-one other detainees were beaten with a pick handle by interrogators this week.

At separate times, and when they were together, the *Sunday Star* men saw at least seven detainees being assaulted in this way by the policemen. They also saw at least 10 incidents in which detainees were punched, slapped, kicked and elbowed. In the worst assaults, victims were required to cling to metal bars while a policeman, wielding the pick handle with both hands, hit them across their buttocks. When the victims fell they were hit and kicked until they rose. When they could no longer stand they were draped over a table while the assault continued. The assaults were seen while the *Star* team was in and around the charge office, out of sight of the cell where the detainees were held.

During their three nights in the cell, the *Sunday Star* team frequently heard screams and crying from the direction of the charge office. Some of the detainees could hardly walk after they had been assaulted, but they had to stand in the cell because it was built to hold only a third of their number.

The *Sunday Star* representatives have signed affidavits about the events and these have been handed to the office of the Commissioner of Police for KwaNdebele. In his affidavit, Jon Qwelane alleges:

"During the time I was in the charge office on Wednesday morning, I witnessed a number of assaults. These are the beatings I witnessed:

"At about 4 A.M., David Masilela, eighteen, was brought into the police station. A plainclothes policeman, who I subsequently learnt was Mahamba, began taking a statement from him. Mahamba slapped David's face several times, saying he must tell the truth about a meeting he had attended to promote class boycotts. David denied attending the meeting.

"While this was happening, William Boshomane, twenty-five, was sitting in a corner of the charge office. He was approached by a policeman called Khanyane. The policeman accused Boshomane of inciting class boycotts, but Boshomane said he was a worker and employed in Rosslyn. Boshomane insisted he had a wife and children to support and had no time for class boycotts, but Khanyane did not believe him. He punched and slapped Boshomane a number of times and said he should tell the truth. Khanyane said to Boshomane, '*Vanaand jy gaan kak, my boytjie.*' (Tonight you're going to shit, my boy.)

"Michael Makua, eighteen, was ordered to the counter and told to hold the bars above it. Mahamba then removed a pick handle from under the counter, and began to beat him with it. After the first blow, which was delivered with two hands from above the shoulder, Makua fell to the floor. He was kicked and slapped, then ordered to stand. Another policeman, Bizana Mthimunye, also slapped Makua. The youth got up and again held on to the bars. The two policemen told him he would tell the truth about a meeting he had attended. But when he denied attending the meeting, Mahamba again swung the pick handle, beating Makua on the buttocks until he fell. This was repeated several times, until Makua could no longer stand. He was then made to lie down on a table. By then, Mahamba and Mthi-

munye had been joined by Khanyane and two other policemen, whose names I do not know, and all five assaulted Makua,
saying he must tell the truth. Makua was screaming loudly and
begging for mercy. After some time, he slipped off the table
onto the floor and the policemen left him alone. He crawled to
the wall and it was clear he was in agony.

"Boshomane was then ordered to the bars. He was similarly
beaten with a pick handle by Mahamba, and with each blow he
collapsed. I saw Mahamba, Mthimunye, Khanyane and the
two other policemen kicking him and ordering him to stand
up. I also recall Khanyane telling Boshomane that if he did not
tell the truth, *'Ons sal jou doodmaak.'* (We'll kill you.) Boshomane was being accused of organizing meetings to promote
class boycotts. He consistently denied the allegations. After he
had fallen to the floor a number of times, I saw Khanyane step
on his groin and the detainee screamed. Mahamba, in order to
stifle the scream, stood on Boshomane's throat and cut off his
breath. Mthimunye and the two other unnamed cops were
kicking Boshomane in the body. When Boshomane gurgled for
breath, Mahamba removed his foot and asked him if he was
going to tell the truth. The detainee insisted he knew nothing
about a meeting to plan boycotts. Khanyane then helped
Boshomane up by his clothes, and hit him hard on the side of
the neck with his fist. The detainee fell again and Khanyane
kicked him again. They then left Boshomane alone and he
crawled to the wall, out of harm's way.

"Just after 7 A.M., on Wednesday, a policeman, Windvoel
Mahlangu, entered the charge office. He walked over to Boshomane and accused him of burning down schools. Mahlangu
reached for the pick handle and told Boshomane to hold the
bars, and then he beat him. Warrant Officer Kruger, acting
station commander, came into the office. He watched as Boshomane was being beaten by Windvoel Mahlangu. I heard Mahlangu tell Kruger that Boshomane was ' *'n groot comrade en is
die leier'* (an important leader of the comrades). I reiterate that
Warrant Officer Kruger was present during Boshomane's beating by Mahlangu.

"Early on Saturday, Johannes Masombuka and another man were brought into the police station and subjected to the pick-handle treatment by Mahamba and Khanyane. They were also beaten when they fell to the floor. I do not have any idea why these people were beaten. Later, when Masombuka and the other man could no longer stand, they were ordered to do press-ups. Mahamba said he wanted fifty press-ups, but the men were clearly in great pain and unable to do as they were ordered, even though they tried. They were then ordered to do situps instead, but again they were unable, having been severely assaulted on their buttocks.

"Later on, a group of policemen entered the charge office half dragging, half carrying a seriously wounded man. The bloodied man, Jabu Mbonani, had a number of gunshot wounds on his body and one on the right-hand side of his face. He appeared very feeble, breathed with difficulty, and could not speak. A fat senior police officer went to the radio transmitter and reported the shooting. This policeman, whom I can identify, then went over to the wounded man, ripped off his vest, and casually counted the gunshot wounds. He disarmed two of the policemen who had brought in the shot man, took one of the firearms, inspected its chambers, and again spoke into the radio. At no stage did I hear anyone summon an ambulance, although I heard one policeman say that this should be done 'in case this person dies.' "

Many journalists have been detained and tortured in South Africa, but this was the first eyewitness report by journalists of the systematic torture of other detainees, and it caused a sensation. The *Sunday Star*'s story was picked up by every major opposition paper (the government press ignored it, as did radio and television), the London *Times,* the *Guardian,* the *Financial Times,* and the *New York Times*. The allegations in the affidavits signed by Qwelane, Mabuza, and Mathe were presented to Brigadier Herzog C. Lerm, KwaNdebele's Police Commissioner. His spokesman, Colonel Andries Kuhn, said, "The KwaNdebele Police appreciate the fact that the *Sunday Star* has brought these allegations to their attention. We will investigate the allegations in depth and if there is any truth in them, appropriate steps will be taken."

The police investigation seemed to go nowhere in the weeks that followed, however, and when the *Star* pressed Brigadier Lerm about whether he had suspended any of the policemen named in the affidavits he said that the assaults reported were "not serious enough" to warrant suspensions. "If it was alleged that they had killed someone," he said, "then I would have suspended them immediately."

Six months later, nothing had yet come of the police investigation in KwaNdebele, and it seemed clear that nothing would. Meanwhile, there was speculation on state-controlled radio that Qwelane and his colleagues and editors might be charged under the Police Act or the Prisons Act after all. But, when I spoke on the phone to Qwelane about it, he seemed less concerned with the chance that he would be prosecuted than with what he had seen in the bantustan jail. "We saw people being forced to admit things that they didn't really do," he said. His voice was unusually slow and urgent. "And I mean people were *clobbered* in there. With every blow, I just felt a shiver. I had never seen anything like it before. Honestly, I don't wish that on my worst enemy."

By most of the standard measures, the intensity of the conflict in South Africa diminished sharply in 1987. In 1986, deaths from political violence averaged more than a hundred a month. The figure shrank to twenty-nine a month for the first nine months of 1987. (The South African Institute of Race Relations, the definitive source for such figures, stopped publishing statistics after September, 1987, because it considered the available information no longer reliable.) In 1986, more than thirty thousand people were detained without trial, and another eleven thousand arrested in unrest-related incidents. By January, 1988, the Detainees' Parents Support Committee estimated that slightly fewer than two thousand people remained in detention without trial. Some of these were being held under permanent security legislation; most were being held under emergency provisions; the distinction between the two types of arbitrary imprisonment was fading, in any case, as the emergency came to seem like a permanent state of affairs.

Two important areas of resistance were not subdued in 1987. Armed attacks, nearly all of them attributed to the ANC, continued at a rate of more than four a week (and the security forces revealed that, for the first time, many of the guerrillas they were catching had received their military training *inside* South Africa). And the black trade unions flourished—the number of strike days recorded in 1987 was the highest ever. International economic sanctions continued to take their toll on the business climate; one analyst in Pretoria said that it seemed that the ANC had decided to try "to make South Africa unprofitable rather than ungovernable."

The extraordinary restrictions on the press have been steadily increased since the beginning of the state of emergency. In December, 1986, a new set of curbs was imposed, barring unauthorized reports of strikes, boycotts, "restricted" meetings, security-force deployments, or court cases involving political detainees. Maximum penalties for violations were fixed at $9,000 in fines and/or ten years in prison. David Steward, of the Bureau for Information, seeking to justify the new regulations, compared the press coverage in South Africa to the press coverage of the Vietnam War, which he said undermined the American military effort there. The definition of a "subversive statement" was expanded under the new curbs to include anything opposing conscription or supporting boycotts, work stayaways, or "alternative structures." Newspapers were also forbidden to indicate that they were being censored.

In the latter part of 1987, the government began threatening to simply close down the *Sowetan,* the *Weekly Mail,* and *New Nation.* The Minister of Home Affairs, Stoffel Botha, described these papers as "the revolution-serving media." He said the *Sowetan* "tended to promote the public image or esteem" of the ANC (which must have been news to the ANC, which had reportedly been so unhappy with the *Sowetan*'s coverage of the

UDF). Botha accused *New Nation* of creating "hatred or hostil-ity" for the security forces by describing police raids as "raids." He also objected to the publication of a picture of ANC president Oliver Tambo, and, replying to a question, said any discussion of Tambo's views on, say, press freedom would also be unaccept-able: "It will elevate Tambo to a status he doesn't deserve." Botha further accused *New Nation* of promoting "the breaking down of public order" by calling for clemency for thirty-two men condemned to death for politically motivated killings.

In 1988, the government closed down *New Nation* for three months, citing advertisements that "implied police torture" in South Africa and articles and photographs that "promoted the image" of the ANC. In May, the Cape Town community news-paper *South,* accused of fueling a "revolutionary climate," was closed down for a month, and in November the *Weekly Mail* was closed for a month. Two more Cape Town papers, *Grassroots* and *New Era,* were closed for three months in February, 1989, also accused of "promoting revolution." The *Weekly Mail*'s sins, Botha said, included promoting the image of the ANC by de-scribing Govan Mbeki, a seventy-seven-year-old former ANC chairman (and former journalist) who was released from prison in November, 1987, after serving twenty-three years of a life sentence for sabotage and treason, as a popular black leader.

The government continued to define black political leaders in its own arcane way. In 1987, P. W. Botha informed Esau Mah-latsi, the "mayor" of Sharpeville, a man who requires police protection from the wrath of his constituents, "People ask me who are the authentic leaders I want to confer with. I am telling you, sir, that you are one of those authentic leaders." Actually, the black leader on whom the government has pinned most of its hopes is Chief Gatsha Buthelezi. Even the state of emergency was deemed not to apply to Buthelezi or to his organization, Inkatha: within weeks of its imposition, permission was granted for a mass Inkatha rally in Soweto, where fifteen thousand men brandished spears and clubs without interference from the po-lice. Buthelezi's claims that he and his followers oppose Pretoria had never looked feebler as tens of thousands of activists disappeared into the regime's jails, and not a single member of Inkatha was detained. Inkatha and its newly launched trade-union federation have continued to operate freely under the emergency, clearly hoping to capitalize on the restrictions under which the UDF and COSATU, its affiliated trade-union federation, suffer. (In late February, 1988, those restrictions became, in the case of the UDF, AZAPO, and fifteen other resistance organizations, absolutely crippling. All were effectively banned. Their assets were not confiscated, but they were barred from all "activity," and many of their leaders were served with individual banning orders. COSATU was also banned from political activity. It was the heaviest crackdown on resistance organizations since October, 1977, when the Black Consciousness movement was destroyed in a wave of bannings.)

Inkatha's attempts to wrest workers and townships away from the UDF have been met, however, with ferocious resistance, and a plan to create a "nonracial" provincial government in Natal, with Buthelezi at its head, collapsed in 1988. Buthelezi's political base seemed to be eroding, and some of his many supporters in the United States and Western Europe began to wonder aloud if a tribal strongman really was the answer to South Africa's crisis. Inside South Africa, the press must wonder very carefully, though, when it comes to Buthelezi. He has sued virtually every opposition newspaper in the country for defamation; an editor at the *Sowetan* estimated, when I spoke to him, that Buthelezi had sued that paper a dozen times for running articles he did not like. And in November, 1987, Buthelezi dragged Denis Beckett, the editor of *Frontline,* into court, claiming twenty thousand rands in damages for an article, reprinted from the *Spectator,* that described him as "nauseatingly pompous and self-important." Buthelezi won the case.

On its home turf in Natal, Inkatha confronted its press problems head-on and, in April, 1987, simply bought the Zulu-language daily, *Ilanga,* from the Argus Company. The paper's editorial staff stopped work in protest after the announcement of the sale. *Ilanga* had a reputation as a courageous, independent paper. It had published an article about corruption in the upper echelons of the KwaZulu government only days before the sale, and its reporters had been threatened and attacked many times by pro-Inkatha vigilantes. According to the *Weekly Mail,* the Argus Company executive who went to speak to the striking journalists at *Ilanga* "was clearly startled at the strong feelings expressed by a united editorial staff. He believed, he told them, that Argus had protected their interests by ensuring medical aid, pension, salaries, and 'work-siting' would remain the same. In any event, he added, he believed the paper basically supported Inkatha—and so did its readers. And then when the protests became voluble, he conceded he neither spoke nor read Zulu, and did not really know what line the newspaper took—if any." The first post-sale issue of *Ilanga* was produced by KwaZulu government employees and featured the entire text of a speech made by Chief Buthelezi after the announcement of the paper's sale to his organization.

More than thirty journalists have been jailed without charges since June, 1986, and many of those who have been released have been slapped with banning orders forbidding them to work in journalism for the duration of the emergency. Zwelakhe Sisulu, who was released in August, 1986, was detained again in December. He spent the next two years in solitary confinement. In July, 1988, he had to be hospitalized for depression. When he was released again in December, 1988, Sisulu was placed under a severe restriction order that prevented his resuming the editorship of *New Nation.* A hunger strike by detainees in early 1989 received international news coverage and forced the release of hundreds of political prisoners, including Brian Sokutu, a freelance journalist from Port Elizabeth. Sokutu had spent more than one thousand days behind bars without being charged. He was placed under severe restrictions after his release. Among those detainees not released was Veliswa Mhlawuli, a reporter for *Grassroots.* Mhlawuli is a thirty-five-year-old mother of two. She was detained on October 5, 1988. On August 19, Mhlawuli had been shot in the face at point-blank range near her home in Cape Town. She had lost her right eye as a result of the attack, and was still under medical treatment when she was detained. As this book goes to press, Mhlawuli has been held incommunicado for more than six months. She has not been charged, and may not even know that her newspaper has been closed by the authorities.

Peter McLean, managing director of the Argus Company, startled opponents of censorship when he announced, in December, 1986, his agreement with the government's depiction of the situation in South Africa. "The public's right to know is of cardinal importance to us," McLean said. "However, we accept that there is a revolutionary attack against this country and that it is of paramount importance that we do not, however unwittingly, give support and encouragement to those seeking to effect change by revolutionary means." This announcement came in response to government demands that newspapers increase self-censorship by sharpening the teeth of an independent disciplinary body called the Media Council. The government press supported the demands, of course, and a few members of the opposition press gave government spokesmen great and sympathetic space in which to explain the latest curbs, but the editors of the major English-language papers rebelled at the prospect of any further collaboration in their own suppression, and in the end the Media Council was left alone. The Media Council's own devotion to the principle of press freedom comes wrapped in a diaphanous garment of political opportunism, however. In July, 1986, the council reported, "Further evidence that an independent Press is a shield against punitive sanctions by the international community was afforded by the American President's public statement that the existence of an independent and outspoken Press in South Africa was one of the factors which enabled him to resist demands for more drastic action in the campaign to pressurize South Africa into reform."

The beleaguering of the international press has continued. More foreign reporters have been kicked out of South Africa, and the incantations of officials like David Steward and Louis Nel—who told reporters in 1986 that "we would like to see all the foreign journalists out of South Africa"—have had an effect. The silence they enforce has had a measurable impact on world interest in the South African crisis. As David Steward explained, "This kind of conflict is a struggle for the hearts and minds of people, and it's a question of creating perceptions."

Just as the perceptions of South Africa created by the international press obsess the apartheid regime, the dangers for ordinary people of speaking to the press—especially the international press—do not subside. In 1987, Godfrey Sicelo Dlomo, an eighteen-year-old civil rights worker in Soweto, gave interviews to Dutch television and to CBS. His remarks about his experiences in detention were used in a CBS News film, *Children of Apartheid,* narrated by Walter Cronkite. Although Dlomo's name was not revealed in the broadcast, the police were able to establish his identity, and they detained him for questioning. Afterward, Dlomo told his mother that the police had threatened his life. In January, 1988, Dlomo was again detained for questioning. Six days after his release, he was found dead in the street. Independent experts said that the course of the bullet that killed Dlomo suggested that he had been kneeling, or in a fetal position, and had been shot from above. Church leaders challenged the government to find the killers—no one has ever been charged in the dozens of assassinations of anti-apartheid workers that have taken place over the years. The police responded by warning Godfrey Dlomo's mother not to speak to the foreign press.

When Bishop Tutu hammered the white South African press in Vienna, he compared its role to the role of the press not in the Vietnam War but in the Rhodesian War, during which, he said, "the media were guilty of a conspiracy of silence, telling white Rhodesians what they thought they wanted to hear." The Rhodesian precedent has become a popular cautionary tale in South Africa. The story, which has been chillingly told in a book called *None But Ourselves,* by Julie Frederikse, shows a press so firmly silenced, so subservient to the embattled white-minority regime, that it eventually acquiesced in the most cynical propaganda schemes to discredit the regime's opponents, twisting and even fabricating news as it sought to persuade its readers that what was happening in the country—a hugely popular liberation struggle—was not happening. The result was a white population taken utterly by surprise when the Zimbabwe independence elections held in 1980 produced a landslide victory for Robert Mugabe, the "terrorist" who whites believed had little real popular support. It is not only black South Africans who cite the Rhodesian experience. White journalists and commentators, including several writing in the *Star,* and some who actually worked on Rhodesian papers during the war there, have been pushing the same analogy.

The analogy is instructive, but it is limited, because there are really no models for what is occurring in South Africa, no precedents. The American civil rights struggle bears some obvious similarities, but that comparison soon breaks down. The equally obvious comparisons to other Third World, particularly African, decolonization struggles are equally inadequate, if only because South Africa differs in basic ways from other African countries. It has a modern industrial economy; its white minority is large and, for all practical purposes, permanent; its geography rules out the possibility of putting a guerrilla army in the field— indeed, the Army is effectively invincible against any foreseeable military threat. No, the South African revolution will have to carve some radically new channels if it is to progress. In fact, while all the African, racial, and colonial elements of the situation limit the relevance of a Marxian model, what is occurring in South Africa may be, nonetheless, the first full-blown proletarian revolution in an industrialized nation that the world has seen.

The South African revolution is not, and probably never will be, a simple matter of the central government falling. Political and economic power is shifting, piecemeal, toward the black majority. In the factories and the mines, black trade unions have grown rapidly in size, strength, and militancy. In the English-language universities, an indigenous school of radical social science, what labor sociologist Edward Webster has called "a social science of liberation," has taken root. Even in the bantustans, black people have been waking up to their own strength: witness the highly effective resistance to "independence" in KwaNdebele. Some of this scattershot insurgency has been opportunistic.

Much of it has been reactive, even spontaneous. But few of the advances have been "top-down" initiatives—conceived, or even condoned, by the state. Most have been "bottom-up"—in defiance of the state. In fact, black protest has tended to rally at precisely those points where the state has attempted to "reform apartheid." Thus, the new constitution promulgated in 1984, which ostensibly "broadened democracy" by creating junior houses of Parliament for people classified "coloured" and Asian, led to the founding of the UDF—initially, to coordinate a boycott of the "coloured" and Asian elections. The reforms that legalized the independent black trade unions have also provided a major opening for the resistance. Conceived as a modernization of labor relations, they now provide what is arguably the most democratic, and certainly the most radical, expression of the black majority's political aspirations.

Each wave of the popular resistance to apartheid has been larger and more powerful than the last. White-minority rule is a vicious anachronism in Africa; it will surely disappear. But how, and how long, it takes to pass from the scene will determine everything about the character of a post-apartheid South Africa. In the near term, the lengthening leash—the near-complete unaccountability—being extended to the security forces and their black allies may well lead to a Lebanon-like stalemate of endemic sectarian violence. The mass imprisonment of UDF leaders has undermined the already-precarious political discipline within the resistance, and the blanket ban on "activity" has driven most forms of protest underground. The government has sought, with some of its recent emergency regulations, to outlaw boycotts entirely. How it can force people *to* use schools, shops, and buses is unclear, but the organization and enforcement of boycotts has, in any case, become effectively impossible. The only large-scale boycotts going today are the township rent boycotts.

A key element of the timetable for change will be the depth of white determination to maintain race rule. There is a tendency within the resistance to dismiss white politics as irrelevant, but the splintering of white solidarity is essential to any realistic scenario for black liberation. The National Party faces challenges from both ultra-conservatives who have left the party and from the liberal opposition. And the positions it is forced to take, while trying to keep its constituency from fleeing in either direction, are devastatingly inconsistent. To voters tempted by the far right, it proclaims the permanence of racial segregation and white rule, and it rejects with contempt all international pressure to dismantle apartheid. Then, to would-be liberals, the regime must turn around and plead its willingness to dismantle apartheid and enter forthwith into negotiations with the black majority. Self-contradictions in the self-contained realm of white politics may seem beside the point to the black masses locked in battle with the white state. But it is the revolutionary pressure from the townships that is driving new wedges into the white body politic, causing splits that ultimately, inevitably, weaken the state.

The conflict in South Africa is often portrayed as a collision of black nationalism and Afrikaner nationalism, a collision to which English-speaking whites, especially liberals, are essentially spectators. It is true that the South African Parliament, where white liberals have long invested the bulk of their political energies, has been marginalized. The PFP leader, Frederick van Zyl Slabbert, conceded as much when he abruptly resigned his position in 1985 and went into extra-parliamentary politics. And in the whites-only elections of May, 1987, the PFP actually lost its status as the official opposition, very likely permanently, to the far-right Conservative Party. (In early 1989, the PFP was folded into a new liberal grouping, the Democratic Party.) But the importance of "big capital," of the Anglo American Corporation and the other owners of the mines and heavy industry, ensures that English-speaking liberals will continue to wield power disproportionate to their numbers or their (lack of) political passion. The passionate "nationalism" of Afrikaners, for that matter, has more to do with the fact that sixty percent of employed Afrikaners work for the state or its subsidiary corporations than it does with dedication to the *volk* or memories of the Boer War. The apartheid bureaucracy is a huge system of Afrikaner political patronage, and the civil service as a whole constitutes an obstacle to change at least as formidable as the military.

Bad conscience will probably never be a major political factor. Each time a report appears showing South Africa to have a human-rights record worse than those of Libya, Cuba, and Zaire, a small shudder seems to run through the white community, but that is all. At the same time, the contributions of the few whites who, motivated by moral or political principle, have identified themselves with the struggle for black liberation—the lawyers, teachers, political organizers, trade unionists, and journalists, many of them associated with the UDF—are important factors in that struggle. This is another way in which the South African conflict differs from the conflict in Rhodesia, where white sympathizers with the black cause were too few to count for much of anything.

Is the comparison between the white South African press today and the Rhodesian press during the war there a fair one? In the case of the government press, and of television and radio, it certainly is. They are clearly collaborating with the apartheid project and will be judged harshly by history. In the case of the opposition press, though, it probably isn't fair. It is an oversimplification that pervades, understandably, the view from the resistance: that all sectors of the white power structure share a common interest in the status quo. If that were true, though, the police would have no reason to tap the *Star*'s phones, or infiltrate its newsroom with informers. If the mainstream press were really such a compliant partner of the state, as resistance leaders often contend, there would be no need, finally, for all the censorship imposed on it.

While the emergency grinds on, the *Star* continues to try to publish unrest reports, some of them provocatively elliptical in their reflection of the restrictions—a boy is dragged between two horses by mysterious forces, a dog shot dead for invisible reasons. The paper's editorials continue to denounce apartheid and the government. In late July, 1986, on the advice of its lawyers, the *Star* even defied the government and published the names of some three thousand detainees. On the other hand, the *Star*'s editors still applaud the Botha government's (increasingly rare) "reform" gestures (Jon Qwelane once asked me, "How do you reform a monster? If you've got a lump of cow dung, and you sprinkle it with all the best herbs from China, it may have a sweeter smell, but it's still cow dung. You still can't eat it"). And they still commend the rebel sports teams that visit South Africa oblivious of the pleas of the resistance that they observe the international sports boycott.

Among the black reporters on the *Star,* four who were there when I was around have since left the paper. Maud Motanyane took an editor's job on a new, white-owned magazine for blacks. Phil Mtimkulu took a post as a lecturer in African history at the University of South Africa, the correspondence college where he earned his degrees. Mike Tissong went to work for the *Sowetan.* And Mudini Maivha, who had wondered if it was time to put away notebooks and take up arms, abruptly fled the country, disappearing in October, 1987, and finally surfacing, nearly two months later, in Zimbabwe, where he went to work for the Pan-Africanist Congress.

In early 1987, the *Star* hired its first black assistant editor, a veteran journalist from Natal who, according to his colleagues in the ghetto, found nothing but frustration in the job. He has since been replaced by a former editor of the *Sowetan.* The *Star*, at the same time, has been "slimming down," per Keith Holt's prescription. "Yes, the paper's a bit tight now," Qwelane said, when I phoned him recently.

Montshiwa Moroke collapsed at work in early 1987. The diagnosis was exhaustion. He was ordered to take some time off. "The Bureau for Information has taken our jobs away from us, but it's still a nerve-racking line of work," Mike Tissong said, the last time we spoke. Strangely enough, on the same day that Moroke collapsed, Qwelane collapsed—from what was later diagnosed as a swollen liver. Qwelane had to have his gall bladder removed. It was not clear whether the new scar could be legitimately added to the tally of his work-related wounds. Something else Qwelane mentioned on the phone: his daughter is not named Tebogo, as he once wished upon a new moon, after all, but Phumla. Phumla is a Zulu word, meaning "a period of rest from toil." The name was Sana's idea, or perhaps Sana's mother's—"I think there was some Third World caucusing behind my back," Qwelane said.

The last time I spoke with Qwelane, he had two pressing matters on his mind. One was MWASA. It seemed that, in October, 1987, while he was out of town on a story, he had been elected, in absentia, chairman of the *Star* local—"unceremoniously pushed into this thankless position" was how he put it. It had become a particularly thankless position since a split had begun developing in the local. At least two of the black reporters on the *Star*—Herbert Mabuza and Mike Siluma—had joined a new, nonracial journalists' union that was affiliated to the UDF. Mabuza, who was still paying his MWASA dues, had even gone to Europe to help promote the new union—which, Qwelane was convinced, had as its main object the destruction of MWASA (because of MWASA's refusal to affiliate to the UDF). "These clowns in the new brigade are regularly at my desk, trying to be pally-pally," Qwelane said. "But I suppose a stand will have to be taken. You cannot run with the hares and hunt with the hounds." Qwelane was hoping to deal with the matter quietly, by simply persuading the defectors to return, but other members of the MWASA leadership were intent upon a confrontation. What Qwelane did not want was "a lot of mudslinging and verbal warfare, because that kind of thing easily spills over into the community."

The other matter on Qwelane's mind was KwaNdebele. He had developed some great sources inside the bantustan, and he was sitting on a terrific story. It seemed that the magistrate whom he and the others had found in the cell where they were jailed in Kwaggafontein had been involved in a case in which George Mahlangu, the new Chief Minister of KwaNdebele, and members of his Cabinet were accused of murder. The killing had taken place when Mahlangu was Minister of Home Affairs. He and the other accused had allegedly set fire to the house of a family that was active in the anti-independence movement. When the family ran from the house, Mahlangu had allegedly thrown a five-year-old boy back into the fire, where he perished. There were eyewitnesses, and an investigation was underway at the time Mahlangu became Chief Minister, but after his inauguration the magistrate had been ordered to call off the investigation. When he refused, he was detained. The chaiman of the KwaNdebele Public Service Commission has also wanted to see the case pursued. He was also detained. Qwelane met him in the cell in Kwaggafontein, too, and that was where he first heard the story.

The KwaNdebele Cabinet still wanted independence for the bantustan, but the continued detention of the magistrate and the bantustan's senior civil servant—not to mention the outstanding murder charges—were making things difficult. When we spoke, Qwelane had just learned that the Cabinet had apparently made a secret trip to Cape Town to see P. W. Botha. The State President had told the Cabinet that there would be no independence until they had put their personal affairs in order. To make sure the Cabinet understood what he meant, Botha had reportedly produced the files on the child-murder case—files which had disappeared from KwaNdebele some time before—from a drawer in his desk.

To nail down this story, Qwelane had decided, he would need to go back to KwaNdebele. His sources in the bantustan were telling him to stay away: the police had been gunning for him, they said, ever since the appearance of his story about the torture of detainees. The *Star*'s editors were also less than enthusiastic. Qwelane was thinking, therefore, about taking a couple of weeks' vacation, and not telling the *Star* where he was going. He already had a "helmet," he said—a mineworker's hard-hat. He figured all he needed now was a pair of greasy overalls, some old boots, a shovel over his shoulder, and a bus ticket out to KwaNdebele. "Then it would just be a question of moving from shack to shack. My private interest is to show the world that these so-called leaders are nothing but thugs, and to stop this bloody nonsense of so-called independence." Qwelane paused, and the transoceanic cables crackled. Then he laughed, deep and smoky. "Ye-e-e-e-es," he said. "I really want this story."

Index

ABC News, 177–178
Aboveground resistance groups. *See*
    AZAPO; UDF
Activists, 64, 65, 134, 223–224
Advertising, 51–52, 123–128
Africa edition, 57, 105, 107, 114, 119,
    148, 205
    circulation, 126
    news selection, 34–35
African languages, 26, 91
African National Congress (ANC). *See*
    ANC
Africans. *See* Blacks
Afrikaans language, 6, 26
Afrikaans-language press, 24–27, 35–36,
    140, 172–173
    and emergency regulations, 172–174
    and National Party, 24–25
    Qwelane and 1976 uprising, 93–94
Afrikaner Weerstandsbeweging (AWB),
    83
Afrikaners, 25, 29, 93–94, 230
Akhalwaya, Ameen, 51, 113, 141
Alexandra, 40–43, 112–113, 134, 188
Americans. *See* United States
ANC, 25, 39, 51, 57, 67, 109, 112, 113,
    116, 154, 199, 202–204, 210, 215,
    222, 228
    and communism, 142, 181
    on press freedom under black rule,
    149
    politics of, 132

strategy of ungovernability, 144–145,
    222
in townships, 50
Anderson, David, 175
Anderson, Ron, 55, 57–58, 161
Anglo American Corporation, 108–109,
    128, 230
Anglo-Boer War of 1899–1902, 29
Angola, 27, 179
Apartheid, 24, 46, 229
    Bantu Education and retribalization
    programs, 91
    Botha on, 27
    current state of, 50–51
    forced removals program, 91
    and migrant labor system, 108
    reforms, 206–207, 228–231
    social, in *Star* newsroom 114–115,
    117–118
Argus Printing and Publishing Company,
    28–29, 33, 97, 108, 114, 176, 202,
    224–225
    and high-potential consumers, 125–126
    legal defense of reporters, 77
Army, 6, 11, 15, 17, 67, 101, 110
    and killings, 119, 203
    military threat to, 228
    seizing of reporter's notes, 118 .
    in townships, 40–41
    and *toyi-toyi* dance, 68
Azanian People's Organization (AZAPO),
    113, 142, 167, 224

from political violence, 50, 221
Catholic mission (KwaNdebele), 11–12, 14–17
CBS News, 177, 226
Censorship. *See* Press; *Star*
Charterists, 132–133
Children of Apartheid news film, 226
Citizen, 25–26, 25–28, 36, 39, 94, 126–127, 177
City Press, 33, 118, 134, 140, 192
and tracing of detainees, 206
Civic associations, 50, 172
Coetzee, J. M., 128
Collaborators, 44–45, 64
Collinge, Jo-Anne, 204–205
"Coloured" people, 8n, 50, 141, 228
Comment radio program, 27
Committee to Protect Journalists, 32, 75
Communism, 67, 142, 183, 191
Community, the, 23
black reporters commitment to, 138–140
Community council system, 50
Community papers, 131, 206
Comrades, 118, 144, 179
in Alexandra, 41–44
description of, 65–66
at funeral services, 64–68
ideology of, 15
in KwaNdebele, 10–12, 15–17, 216, 219
against middle-class blacks, 148
and pressure on *Sowetan*, 134–136
protection payments to, 228
Qwelane on, 89–90
tsotsis posing as, 136–137
Congress of South African students, 43
Congress of South African Trade Unions (COSATU), 134, 188, 224
Conservative Party, 229–230
COSATU. *See* Congress of South African Trade Unions
The Cosby Show television show, 26, 100
Courts, 51, *See also* People's courts
Cowell, Alan, 179
Cronkite, Walter, 226
Crossroads squatters camp, 138, 179

Dalling, Dave, M. P., 182
Darnton, John, 179
De Vos, Wim, 177
Dé Ath, George, 138
Democracy, 133, 171
Detainees
in KwaNdebele prison, 218–221
Star listing of, 231
tracing of, 206

Detainees' Parents Support Committee, 156–158, 221
Detentions, 168–172, 199–201, 203, 206
by 1988, 221–222
Die Burger, 24, 173
Die Transvaler, 24, 29, 173
Die Vaderland, 35, 172
Die Volksblad, 173
Dlomo, Godfrey Sicelo, 226–227
Dompas (identification card), 207
Drum magazine, 73, 93–94
and Qwelane, 94–95
Duduza, 76–77, 201
Dutch Reformed Church, 24, 26

East Rand funerals, 62–69
Eastern *Star*, 29
Editors. *See also* names of editors; *Star*
and black reporters, 23, 105–119
of *Ilanga*, 224–225
Education, 50, 51, 91
black reporters and English ability, 90–92, 106–107
Emerald, 193–194
Emergency, state of, 3, 31, 167–183
developments since 1986, 221–227, 231
first few days and author's experiences, 187–195
goals and regulations, 170–172, 192, 217, 229
English language, 6
and black reporters, 90, 106–107
Qwelane and, 90–92
English-language newspapers, 24, 28–36. *See also* Press; *Star*
and Anglo interests, 108–109
anti-Afrikaner rule, 29–30
black extra editions, 33–35, 148
black leaders criticism of, 35–36, 202
black readership of, 146–147
and black reporter tradition, 73
daily circulation, 28
editorial stance, 111–113
government censorship and bannings, 31–32
and Media Council, 226
owners of, 28–29
police and government intimidation, 32
pro-government *Citizen*, 25–28, 36, 39, 94, 177
reaction to emergency, 174–177, 202
salaries paid, 115
Equal opportunity, 111
at *Star*, 106
Ethnic states, 8–9. *See also* Bantustans
Europe, 99, 123–124, 179–180, 224